D0970508

HIGH
IMPACT
H.I.M.M.
MIDDLE
MANAGEMENT

Solutions for Today's
Busy Managers

By Lisa Haneberg

Adams Media
Avon, Massachusetts

To Bill
You are my rock and sunshine.

Copyright ©2005 by Lisa Haneberg.
All rights reserved. This book, or parts thereof, may not be reproduced
in any form without permission from the publisher; exceptions
are made for brief excerpts used in published reviews.

Published by
Adams Media, an F+W Publications Company
57 Littlefield Street, Avon, MA 02322. U.S.A.
www.adamsmedia.com

ISBN: 1-59337-158-6

Printed in the United States of America.

J I H G F E D C B A

Library of Congress Cataloging-in-Publication Data
Haneberg, Lisa.
H.I.M.M. / Lisa Haneberg.
p.   cm.
ISBN 1-59337-158-6
1. Middle managers. 2. Organizational effectiveness. 3. Executive ability.
I. Title: High impact middle management. II. Title: HIMM. III. Title.
HD38.2.H25 2004
658.4'3—dc22
2004013565

This publication is designed to provide accurate and authoritative information with regard to
the subject matter covered. It is sold with the understanding that the publisher is not engaged
in rendering legal, accounting, or other professional advice. If legal advice or other expert
assistance is required, the services of a competent professional person should be sought.
—From a *Declaration of Principles* jointly adopted by a Committee of the American Bar
Association and a Committee of Publishers and Associations

Many of the designations used by manufacturers and sellers to distinguish their
products are claimed as trademarks. Where those designations appear in this book
and Adams Media was aware of a trademark claim, the designations have been
printed with initial capital letters.

Interior illustrations © 2000 Artville, LLC.

This book is available at quantity discounts for bulk purchases.
For information, call 1-800-872-5627.

Contents

Foreword

IT HAS BEEN TEN YEARS since *Flight of the Buffalo,* the book that Jim Belasco and I wrote together, was published. These ten years have provided a lot of time to study and reflect on the ideas and principles espoused in that book. An active career as the CEO of a large, rapidly growing company and as a coach to leaders of other companies has provided many opportunities to test and refine my beliefs about what it takes to create an organization that continually performs at a high level.

We know that people are what make the difference in an organization. Their performance determines the performance of the organization. Great people make great companies. But what makes people great? That is what my book was about—helping leaders to create an environment that helps and encourages people to rise to greatness. The question I have been pondering since that book is a more difficult one. What keeps people great over a period of time?

What I have found is that greatness doesn't just happen. People and organizations learn how to become great through constant effort. The few people who maintain their greatness over many years have learned to focus on becoming great, not on being great.

It is that focus on becoming that keeps people learning and growing even though their performance is already at an extraordinary level.

Tiger Woods didn't start out great. He learned how to become great through many years of training both his mind and his body. This resulted in a great victory at the Masters, where he won with a record margin. Shortly after that victory, he realized that he had flaws in his swing that would prevent him from reaching his goal of being the greatest golfer in history. He spent the greater part of a year removing those flaws and has since played at a much higher level. I suspect that, even now, he is working on ways to once more widen the gap between him and his competitors. Lisa Haneberg is very much like Tiger. She is driven to continuously learn and improve her effectiveness. We first met while working together to create high-performing leadership teams at a division of the Mead Paper Company. Her work there was outside the ordinary for a human resources person and it had a huge impact on her company. This work served as a springboard for her learning about performance, which she has doggedly pursued to this day. *H.I.M.M.: Solutions for Today's Busy Managers* is a result of that work.

H.I.M.M.: Solutions for Today's Busy Managers is a very important contribution to the study of organizational effectiveness because it focuses on the people who are the key to any organization's performance: the people in the middle. These are the people whose efforts determine the success of any endeavor. Leaders can design wonderful strategies, but the success of the organization resides in the execution of those strategies. The people in the middle are the ones who make it work. Based on all of the companies I've seen, including my own, I'll take an average strategy that is extremely well executed over a great strategy with mediocre execution every time. That is why we spend a substantial amount of our development efforts on this group of individuals at my company. We know who drives our performance.

That is why this book is so valuable. When Lisa first asked me to write this foreword, she sent me the book to read. I found a number of excellent development concepts in it when I read it, so I gave it to our personnel development department. They found the book very helpful and have incorporated a number of concepts into work at Johnsonville Sausage. We think it will be very helpful in our efforts to become the best sausage company in the world. I am sure you will also find value in it.

Ralph C. Stayer
CEO & Owner
Johnsonville Sausage, Inc.
Entrepreneur, Consultant/Coach, Author
Author of Flight of the Buffalo: Soaring to Excellence, Learning to
    Let Employees Lead

Acknowledgments

THE HIGH IMPACT MIDDLE MANAGEMENT SYSTEM has developed over many years and with the participation and cooperation of hundreds of middle managers. My thanks to all the managers I have had the honor to work with at Black & Decker, Mead Paper, Intel, Amazon.com, and Cruise West. Special thanks go to the managers I worked very closely with, including Barry Kelly, Dave Borden, Jeff Hedges, John Underwood, Johna Campbell, Jim Booth, Denny Wormington, Dave Giblin, John Pemberton, Jeff Krida, Kate Mulqueen, Jerre Fuqua, Timo Shaw, Melanie Cole, Martha Wharton, and Karin Thompson. You have shaped my thinking and this book. I am also grateful to Ralph Stayer, CEO of Johnsonville Sausage, for his inspiration, coaching, and support over the past ten years and for writing the foreword.

This book could not have become a reality without several people who believed in the manuscript and me. I would like to thank my agent, Jeff Herman, for his unwavering support and confidence in this book. You are a real pro and I am fortunate to have you on my side. A special thanks also goes to my editor, Jill Alexander, who saw the potential of this book and then guided me through the publishing process. Your influence and participation in this project has made the book richer. Thanks to the many Adams Media folks who have fashioned this book into its current form. Your work is beautiful. I would also like to thank Elizabeth Lyon for the great coaching and guidance that enabled me to create a winning book proposal. I am also indebted to my publicists, Rick Frishman and Brian Feinblum of Planned TV Arts, for helping me gain exposure and voice with the media.

Finally, I must acknowledge my wonderful husband, Bill, who selflessly gave his time and support to me throughout the book's creation.

Introduction

IN ANY ORGANIZATION, there are two kinds of middle managers. There are those who get the work done but never think beyond what needs to be completed in the short term. They rush from one task to another, never quite recognizing which is most important to their company's larger objectives. Though they may work hard and have good intentions, they fail to see the big picture and, thus, add little value to their organization or the functions they manage. Then there are high impact middle managers. High impact middle managers see the big picture. They know how to manage operational practices and execute tactical goals to support strategic initiatives. They add value to their organization and thus elevate their position from that of middle man to key player.

There is an almost magical synergy in a work environment when a high impact middle manager operates at peak efficiency. Their questions are timely and on target; their ideas are provocative in ways that help move the work forward. They know how to think strategically. Transitions from one task to the next seem choreographed. As they walk through the office, their demeanor is calm but with a sense of urgency. Busy, focused, and driven, these managers produce results and imbue the workplace with energy. Those who watch these managers may feel motivated or intimidated—but they are not unaffected.

Although their days are full, they have more time at their disposal than other middle managers who produce less. That's because effective middle managers use tiny pockets of time to accomplish big things. They plan well and anticipate whatever is coming their way. When they do make a mistake, they quickly solve the problem and learn from the experience. These middle managers are effective because they understand what they need to do, methodically do those things, and adjust quickly and proactively when barriers pop up or conditions change.

Unfortunately, most middle managers have never experienced this kind of productivity. They spend their days trying to catch up, never mind moving ahead. Barriers and challenges bring their productivity to a grinding halt. They focus on the urgent rather than the important. Disconnected by a lack of communication with their peers and managers, their work is no longer aligned to achieve results, and team members lose sight of how their work influences the organization or why it even matters. Results suffer because the middle manager and his or her team are not set up to deliver them.

It is heartbreaking to see smart, hardworking, and well-meaning managers fail. Unfortunately, in today's ever-changing and competitive work environment, it happens all too often. Success is most difficult for middle managers because their role is more complicated and challenging than the roles of either frontline supervisors or senior executives. Even so, middle managers can experience peak performance with the right guidance, development, and support. To do so, they need to learn the craft of middle management and overcome several challenges that can wreck their capacity to perform.

A great middle manager—referred to in this book as a *high impact middle manager*—is an individual who makes substantial qualitative and quantitative contributions to his or her organization and moves work forward with velocity and direction. The high impact middle manager can straddle several planning periods to address the needs of today, this week, this month, this year, and the next few years. He or she understands the difficult and complex nature of his or her role and feels energized by being the conduit linking corporate thought, action, and results. High impact middle managers "get it." They know that their job is the most exciting for those who relish being in the thick of things.

This book offers a vision of high impact middle management and a system for achieving this superior level of performance.

High Impact Middle Management, or H.I.M.M., is a management system created to provide busy middle managers with an integrated set of practices and techniques that maximize results and success. This is a distinct system because it addresses corporate execution and success from the perspective of middle management. H.I.M.M. recognizes that middle management is the engine for corporate results and offers regimens and practices to ensure performance.

Who Is a Middle Manager?

Depending on the size of the company, middle managers may hold the title of vice president, director, or manager. Middle-management positions are responsible leadership posts typically two to seven layers below the president. They may have other supervisors or managers reporting to them and are responsible for managing at least one function within the company. Middle managers are not CEOs, but are high enough up the corporate ladder that they are expected to understand and take part in creating business plans, budgets, and other planning documents.

The Motivation for This Book

Middle managers have a more direct impact on business results than any other layer of an organization does; it is vital, therefore, that they receive the resources and development they need. Sadly, there are few books or training programs targeted to meet the unique needs of middle managers. This is unacceptable and a serious concern because businesses suffer when middle managers do not know what to do. As the glue that bonds corporate strategy to work productivity, middle managers can either enable or impede corporate accomplishment. Developed and perfected over many years, the observations, tools, and suggestions that make up the H.I.M.M. system have helped many middle managers do their jobs better. This book is one of the few that explains and illustrates successful middle-management practices and tools. Its goal is to share the H.I.M.M. system of management in a way that is clear and easy to implement. Middle managers who incorporate this system into their daily practices will receive a payoff of improved management skills, better results, and increased promotability. Implementing H.I.M.M. will enable you to enjoy your job more fully, see better results, and experience peak performance from yourself and your team.

How the Book Is Organized

This book offers a comprehensive look at the challenges and opportunities that middle managers face in today's business climate. Each part addresses a dimension, or layer, of the middle manager's job. Part 1 focuses on helping you to fully understand and appreciate your important role as middle manager. Part 2 offers techniques for planning and measuring results and performance. Part 3 looks at how structure and time can enable or hinder your success and defines practices that will help you improve your productivity. Performance optimization and leadership are at the heart of Part 4. In Part 5 you will learn how to fully utilize the techniques included in this book.

While the information in each chapter and part can be read and applied separately, you will find the techniques to be complementary and additive in nature. The more you try and use, the greater your results will be. Please enjoy the book's chapters in the order that addresses your needs the best; however, I do recommend reading Part 1 prior to other sections, as it explains the foundations and assumptions of the H.I.M.M. system.

Part One

H.I.M.M.—A Powerful Force for Executing Results

Chapter 1

High Impact Middle Management and the H.I.M.M. System

THE NUMBERS WERE IN. Black & Decker had regained the market share they had lost over the past several years—and then some. The company's new DeWalt line of power tools had made it to the marketplace in record time and to rave reviews. It was a great lineup. The tools represented cutting-edge technology, and they were beautifully designed and expertly packaged. Cross-functional international product development teams had worked tirelessly on the DeWalt line design, development, and launch for over two years. Their hard work paid off big for Black & Decker, giving them the boost in the marketplace that they sorely needed. Everyone involved in the DeWalt launch knew they had been part of something special.

It would be hard to argue that the DeWalt strategy and vision of producing a superior line of tools for the serious do-it-yourselfer and professional user was not brilliant; it set the stage for the right work to happen. The inspiring strategy got the team started, but what made the

3

DeWalt plan execution so successful was the quality of Black & Decker's middle managers. In the end, it was high impact middle management that produced breakthrough results and put Black & Decker back on the map as a major player in the competitive do-it-yourself power-tool market. How did they do it?

- They were extraordinarily good project managers.
- They had an uncompromising attitude about hiring only the best for the DeWalt team.
- They practiced effective cross-functional and international communication.
- They established an environment that encouraged creativity and innovation.
- They planned well and made sure that priorities were clear.
- They communicated the vision of senior executives with passion and clarity.

Black & Decker's team of high impact middle managers did outstanding work and made a significant contribution to a companywide achievement. That is high impact middle management in action.

What Middle Managers Do

Middle managers are the fundamental link tying an organization's strategies to the people and projects needed to produce results. They are the folks in the middle who see and manage how various parts of the enterprise work. It's a big and often underestimated responsibility. **FIGURE 1.1** shows what the typical middle manager's role might look like. On the top portion of the model, various concerns converge and compete for a middle manager's time and attention. These concerns include a broad range of tasks such as planning, goal setting, performance management, problem solving, process improvement, relationship building, analysis, communication updates, budgeting, and decision-making. Barriers and mucky muck (see Chapter 6) can block these items from getting the time and consideration they deserve.

Fig. 1.1—The typical middle manager's role

The funnel represents the distillation process that middle managers must use to decide how they spend time and complete their work. Middle managers are like a corporate funnel, interpreting and translating strategies, needs, and choices for their team. They practice techniques and make decisions that influence results. Ineffective work practices and barriers can combine to slow output to a trickle.

Fig. 1.2—A middle manager using H.I.M.M.

FIGURE 1.2 shows what results can look like when managers use the High Impact Middle Management system, or H.I.M.M. The results are much better! H.I.M.M. helps middle managers deal with daily tasks and strategic demands while providing tools to reduce barriers to productivity. Middle-management areas of concern that H.I.M.M. addresses include:

- Constructing paradigms that best serve execution and results
- Fostering collaboration to improve results and efficiency
- Determining team performance
- Setting goals for peak performance
- Dealing with daily obstacles to results
- Removing factors that limit throughput
- Managing time
- Learning process-alignment techniques
- Learning performance-management techniques
- Acquiring skills for coaching others
- Using the H.I.M.M. system to improve results
- Honing middle-management skills to build your career

By using H.I.M.M., you will save time and resources by focusing your efforts in areas where they can have the greatest impact. In addition, this book presents a number of techniques that can facilitate breakthroughs—those quantum-leap improvements that can happen quickly and ignite results.

The Guiding Principles of the H.I.M.M. System

Every management system is built on a set of assumptions and principles. These values form the foundation for each philosophy, technique, and tool included in the system. The H.I.M.M. system was designed with several basic principles in mind. These principles speak to what is unique about middle management and how middle managers produce great results. These guiding principles apply to organizations of any size or any industry. In addition to providing a theoretical backdrop for the system, the guiding principles of High Impact Middle Management can be a powerful catalytic tool when used as part of a middle manager's definition of success (see Chapter 2).

Principle #1: Being a middle manager is exciting.

In almost any company, the most challenging and rewarding jobs will be in middle management. Why? Because middle managers are close to the action but also take part in shaping the future strategy and direction of the company. Top executives rarely get to see the action that middle managers do, and they also have to deal with more bureaucracy and politics. Frontline managers get the action but rarely help determine the company's future. As a middle manager, you have your finger on the pulse of the company and can make things happen. Senior executives trust talented middle managers to implement the vision and deliver on the business proposition. And because in most companies there are several layers of middle management, most middle managers can enjoy the benefits of this fascinating work while progressing in their career.

Principle #2: Middle management is a craft.

The middle manager's job is complex and dynamic and requires focus to deliver results. Weighing competing demands, and making choices about how to manage time, takes practice and development. As managers grow and mature, they hone their craft and create a style that is effective and unique to them. Along the way, they also learn techniques and practices via mentoring, training, and coaching. The purpose of this book is to help you hone your management skills.

Principle #3: Great managers do what others don't or won't.

A middle manager's job is littered with tasks that are undesirable, tiring, mundane, or even frightening. Great managers do things that others put off or ignore. Mediocre managers don't. Not everyone likes to counsel employees or create work plans, but these tasks are necessary and time-sensitive.

Principle #4: Beliefs determine behavior.

Managers do what they think about most and based on what they believe to be true. Their actions come from a set of beliefs formed about job responsibilities, expectations, and reinforcement. To affect a different result, you will need to adopt a different mindset. Breakthroughs can occur when beliefs line up to get the desired outcome.

Principle #5: Relationships influence results.

Relationships developed with team members, peers, managers, and customers are important. If you discount relationships, you won't garner the cooperation and support you need from others to produce ideal results—and you are more likely to see your career derail. Great managers develop and maintain positive relationships. Managers who are poor team players, or unpleasant to work with, are less successful. Many eventually lose their jobs and most will not progress far. The old admonition rings true here: never burn bridges.

Principle #6: Managerial strengths and weaknesses are known.

People notice who is charismatic, who gets defensive, and whether someone is likely to pass the buck. Management is public work, noticed by employees and coworkers every day. Everyone knows who the best negotiator is and who the underperformer is. Because strengths and weaknesses are known, there is no disadvantage to openly discussing them. As a manager, you have a choice to make. You can take an interest in and deal with development needs or ignore them and hope no one notices. The latter strategy is flawed because people *do* notice. The only practical and helpful approach is to see faults and failings for what they are and openly discuss them so improvement can occur. Managers should never want to be the last to know if they have a personality trait that is driving people nuts or derailing the work. Managers who acknowledge the areas where they need to improve will enjoy more support and respect from others than those who do not.

Principle #7: Great middle management can be learned, but one must "get it."

Middle management is a craft, a set of practices, and a job that managers can learn with the right training and guidance. Good middle managers are cultivated, not born. Great managers come in wildly different styles and personalities. However, it is essential that all middle managers fully understand their jobs and accountability. Managers who don't take on their role are not likely to succeed, and often see their careers stall or atrophy.

Principle #8: Middle managers exist to make things happen.

Middle managers are not there to simply oversee what is going to occur on its own. They make a huge difference and play a vital role in improving the business. It is in the face of defeat, during an impending failure, or on the verge of an exciting opportunity that a middle manager's role kicks into high gear. Great middle managers know they exist to make a positive difference, and seek out opportunities to make an impact.

These eight guiding principles are reinforced throughout the H.I.M.M. system and this book. H.I.M.M. is for professional managers who are interested in new or different techniques that will make their work more fruitful, and who want to make a difference.

H.I.M.M. Generates Results

H.I.M.M. builds middle-management capacity by developing results-oriented responses, or RORs. These RORs are enablers that can have an immediate effect on work. Each H.I.M.M. component reinforces and supports the others so that as you integrate H.I.M.M. into your management regimen, results will improve at a more significant rate than if you implemented them separately. As you develop your ability to apply RORs in one area, you will also learn skills that will enable you to handle other tasks more effectively. For example, developing dialogue skills for goal setting will also aid you in your ability to use dialogue to improve processes. An ROR is not a technique itself, but it influences how a technique is used.

The following table lists several of the RORs that H.I.M.M. uses. Results will vary based on choices made about what to do and how to spend time. RORs are listed on the left side of the model and Low-Results Responses (LRRs) on the right side. Responses on the left side produce better results. Managers who are dissatisfied with their results can look through this model to discover how to improve their responses.

Results-Oriented Responses Versus Low-Results Responses

RORs	LRRs
Being an Owner: Assumes responsibility for the outcome. Takes initiative to make things better. Does whatever it takes to get ideal results. Heart is committed and mind is engaged.	Being a Custodian: Does only what is required. Waits for others to act. Hopes someone else will take ownership. Avoids that which is unpleasant. Behavior is compliant. Heart and mind not fully engaged.
Being Active: Takes the initiative to get things done. Is not easily deterred by setbacks. Proactive. When barriers are present, immediately identifies them and implements an alternative action plan.	Being Passive: Won't take action unless told to do so. Acts only when necessary. Reactive in stance and style. Barriers and setbacks result in inaction.
Generating: Able to generate new and better alternative approaches and carry them out. Creates from unlimited possibilities. Does not get stuck on how things are already being done.	Being Automatic: Sticks with the way things have always been done; preserves the status quo. Prefers to act by habit and won't move out of his/her comfort zone. Does not create new approaches or solutions.
Keeping Promises: Does what is promised. Fulfills commitments. Keeps his or her word.	Broken Promises or Commitments: Does not follow through with what he/she has promised or committed to. Lets to-do items build up beyond the date expected. Does not follow through on real or implied agreements.
Influencing Through Enrollment: Influences others by having them see, understand, and take ownership of the goal for themselves. Demonstrates the strategy and plan in such a way that others see and take on the vision for themselves. Others are committed and passionate about the vision and plan.	Influencing Through Subtle Coercion: Communicates the vision and plan in a way that resembles a direction or a suggestion. Influences others by making them feel they need to accept and conform. This type of influencing others rarely results in committed and passionate performance.

»»

Results-Oriented Responses Versus Low-Results Responses *(continued)*

RORs	LRRs
Being Service Oriented: Sees his or her role as one that provides service to others. Facilitates cooperation, commitment, and learning. Manages from the mindset, "What can I do to help others excel today?"	Expecting to Be Served: Sees his or her role as one in which people should serve him or her. This stance limits the capacity to have impact on others. Manages from the mindset, "What have you done for me today?"
Being Coachable: Accepts and uses feedback, input, criticism, and ideas from others without getting defensive. Recognizes that others have something to offer to the process.	Being Uncoachable: Blocks the environment from being influential; puts up barriers. Focuses more on being right, looking good, and appearing in charge.
Practicing Quality Dialogue: Communicates with the intent of making a difference or moving a topic forward. Engages in active conversation focused on the topic at hand.	Using Dialogue Without Purpose: Communicates in a way that does not move the topic forward. Spends time discussing rumors, gossip, complaints, diversions, whining, and opinions not helpful toward enabling the desired result.

These RORs can help you focus your time and energy where it will yield the highest benefit (see the sidebar on the 80/20 rule on page 15). A quick review of the list of RORs can help get a stalled project or goal moving again. RORs, guiding principles, and a respect for the important and complex nature of the middle manager's job are central to the H.I.M.M. system. They come together to help middle managers improve their performance, results, and career success.

How to Apply RORs to Everyday Middle-Management Challenges

Steve struggled to understand why the marketing materials produced by his department did not capture the essence of the company's products. He was also frustrated by the fact that while his team members always seemed busy, they were not completing the most important work, such as ensuring quality of the materials. Was the writing not compelling enough? Were the pictures not good enough? Did the layout fail to convey the right message? All of these areas were part of the problem, but the underlying cause of the quality problem was less specific. How was Steve approaching the problem? Were his responses likely to lead to success or failure? Reviewing just a few items on the list of RORs sheds some light on his situation:

- Being an Owner—Steve owned his role as functional leader, but he also let the fact that he inherited the process slow down his improvement of it. There was an opportunity for him to improve results by taking more ownership of how he wanted the department to run currently—rather than going with the status quo.
- Being Active—Steve had implemented a few small ideas and new actions. However, he would have realized more significant improvements if he had taken action in a more meaningful way.
- Generating—Steve was a very creative manager, so generating new ideas would not have been a problem . . . if it weren't for the issue of people. He allowed his preconceptions of what the current team players would accept or reject to curtail his natural tendency to be a creative problem solver.

By looking at just three RORs, Steve could create several potential approaches for how to improve the production process. H.I.M.M. uses the elegant simplicity of the RORs as a basis for each specific technique. As you review each suggestion, you can return to the list of RORs and see how it ties in to at least one preferred response.

The 80/20 Rule

》》 In the early 1900s, economist Vilfredo Pareto established the Pareto principle, otherwise known as the 80/20 rule. He found that 20 percent of the population owned 80 percent of the land in Italy. He then noticed that this ratio applied to other things in science, business, and life. The 80/20 rule asserts that 20 percent of work performed will account for 80 percent of results. Conversely, the other 80 percent of the work will yield only 20 percent of the results. Thus, a few actions will make a greater proportional impact. The 80/20 rule is also used to evaluate errors and problems; therefore, the top 20 percent of systemic problems cause 80 percent of the inefficiencies.

The H.I.M.M. system applies the 80/20 rule (see sidebar) to many aspects of middle management. Just a few methods practiced together will make a significant impact on results and execution. H.I.M.M. focuses on the 20 percent of effort that will yield 80 percent of impact for busy middle managers. H.I.M.M. highlights the 20 percent of actions that matter most.

The H.I.M.M. system was built on the premise that a middle manager's job is challenging, complex, and very important to a corporation's success. As a middle manager, you have the opportunity to do work that is meaningful and exciting. The right training and development can help frustrated or unsuccessful middle managers become high impact middle managers. Unfortunately, most middle managers are so busy and overwhelmed that they are not likely to take the time to attend training. That is a shame because mastering middle management is much easier with good coaching and guidance. The H.I.M.M. system presented in this book will teach time-pressed middle managers what they can do differently that will offer the greatest benefit to their team and their organization.

Chapter 2

How to Think Like a High Impact Middle Manager

THE WAY IN WHICH a middle manager approaches a situation can either help or hinder the results he or she is seeking. Thoughts and beliefs can limit opportunities or, conversely, enable options to be discovered and considered. High impact middle managers select beliefs that support their goals. When thinking is aligned with the larger objective, productive actions naturally happen and lead to positive results.

Success Stories

There are many well-known business success stories that illustrate the power of aligning beliefs to company goals. A belief may seem like a tiny, inconsequential thing, but it can get an organization rolling in the right direction. The reverse is also true. Stagnant thinking that is not aligned to goals can contribute to the downfall of a company or department.

Here are a few examples of successful leaders who recognized the importance of beliefs and how they impact business results.

More than sausage

"If it is to be, it is up to me. If it is up to me, it shall be." Thousands of managers have heard Ralph Stayer, CEO of Johnsonville Sausage, say these words during talks at corporations around the world. Johnsonville Sausage has enjoyed significant and lasting success with Stayer at the helm. The company is famous for its bottom-up, top-down integration of ownership and innovation that creates the best and most popular sausage products on the market today. In his best-selling business book *Flight of the Buffalo,* Stayer describes the importance of productive thoughts and the breakthroughs he experienced by aligning his beliefs for success. "I learned to change from being a victim to being responsible by asking myself, 'What am I doing or not doing that causes the situation I don't like?' Restating the problem into factors that I control helps me feel, and be, powerful." Part of Stayer's leadership mantra is to first assume "I am the problem," and then approach each improvement opportunity from there.

Direct to you

In his book *Direct from Dell,* Michael Dell wrote, "Our success is due, in part, to not just an ability, but a willingness, to look at things differently. I believe opportunity is part instinct and part immersion—in an industry, a subject, or an area of expertise. Dell is proof that people can learn to recognize and take advantage of opportunities that others are convinced don't exist. You don't have to be a genius, or a visionary, or even a college graduate to think unconventionally. You just need a framework and a dream." Michael Dell started his computer company in 1984 with $1,000 and a dream to one day be as big as IBM. By 1998, the Dell Computer Corporation was taking in $18 billion in sales over the Internet each year, and by 2004, the Dell Computer Corporation was number 31 on the *Fortune* 500 list with over $41 billion in revenues. The Dell business model changed the way all computer manufacturers do business, including how they go to market, manage inventory, and produce products.

Delivery you can count on

"Back in 1971 my belief was that you could run these small, high-value-added computer parts through this hub-and-spoke system. Also, I did something else a little bit unusual, which was to combine the airplanes and trucks into one delivery system. This didn't seem to me to be so controversial, but all the traditional people felt that it was highly iconoclastic. So that's the genesis of Federal Express." This is how Fred Smith, CEO of FedEx, described the thinking behind this successful business launch in 1971 in a recent *Fortune* magazine article. Over the last three decades, FedEx has revolutionized the shipping business. Smith believed the shipping business could work in the same way banks clear checks: through a hub-and-spoke system. By applying this model to shipping, FedEx delivered on a promise of service consistency, speed, and accuracy. Since the launch of FedEx, UPS and the United States Postal Service have come out with similar services to match the breadth of shipping choices, reliability, and efficiency that FedEx has achieved.

Turning Beliefs into Results

Each of these stories illustrates how powerful, positive, and focused beliefs lead to favorable results. These examples show how thoughts affect actions. By adopting beliefs that served their goals, Stayer, Dell, and Smith produced outstanding results. Successes, a few setbacks, and a drive to continue the move forward characterized their journeys. Some of their beliefs have remained the same whereas others have changed as needed to serve their goals. These CEOs know that how they approach running their businesses has contributed to their successes. They are not alone. High impact middle managers use these same principles to get results.

When results are lacking, the first thing to look at are the underlying beliefs that are driving your actions. The relationship between beliefs and actions is significant and cyclical. Actions come from beliefs, and in turn, actions and results reinforce beliefs. This cycle can either help or hinder success. **FIGURE 2.1** is an example of how this belief-action cycle can get in the way of results.

Beliefs
This is the way it's always been
This is not my issue
I am already working too hard
I am burned out
I should not stick out my neck

Results
Managerial work is stressful and draining
Senior management applies pressure to improve results
Nothing changes
It takes more work to maintain current productivity
Results suffer

Actions
Sticks with status quo
Does not initiate new solutions
Discourages team members from taking the initiative

Fig. 2.1—A typical belief-action cycle

Notice how the cycle reinforces the status quo and increases the manager's levels of stress and frustration. **FIGURE 2.2** depicts a more productive belief-action cycle.

Fig. 2.2—The H.I.M.M. belief-action cycle

This model shows how helpful beliefs lead to productive actions and improved results. These results reinforce proactive and positive beliefs. The difference between beliefs that serve a manager's goals and those that do not is easy to distinguish when examined closely.

High impact middle managers get better results by taking on a set of beliefs, called a *definition of success,* that will be most useful and abandoning beliefs or mindsets that will not serve them well. All managers have a definition of success, and it is important to know whether your definition is helping you and your team get where you want to go or getting in the way. High impact middle managers have a definition of success that leads to ideal results and personal satisfaction.

Examining Your Inner Beliefs

People spend most of their waking hours in conversation—not with others, but with themselves. The mind, on both conscious and unconscious levels, is constantly processing internal chatter, or self-talk. The internal dialogue that is most critical for a manager regards the beliefs he or she holds about accomplishment and failure.

These messages are particularly powerful because they shape the choices you make and the way in which you look at your job. Imagine what would happen if you believed that being strong or authoritative meant winning arguments at any cost. You would probably act like an obnoxious control freak and alienate others. This would not yield good results. If another middle manager adopted the belief that disagreements should be handled in a manner that preserves and strengthens business relationships, then he or she would approach things very differently—and the results would be more productive. When managers examine and realign their definition of success, they can experience improved results and perhaps an immediate breakthrough.

What Is Your Definition of Success?

Your definition of success is the collection of beliefs you hold that impact how you choose to manage. These beliefs determine how you will approach making decisions, which activities you will tend to favor and those you might avoid. They also influence how you react during times of stress, failure, success, and creativity.

- Beliefs about how success is achieved
- Beliefs about what success looks like
- Beliefs about what is expected

- Beliefs reinforced by past successes and failures
- Comparative assumptions about what has made others successful
- Beliefs, whether positive or negative, passed on by your role models
- Beliefs not readily admitted or recognized until examined in detail
- Beliefs that can be changed instantaneously

As a middle manager, you should regularly evaluate and realign your definition of success. While this may seem straightforward, the process can be tricky because some beliefs are unknown or not recognized. It is common, for example, to verbally define success as one thing and then behave in a contrary way. Verbally, a manager might say that success means achieving results for the benefit of the company and its employees, while behaviorally he or she indicates that success means being right and in control.

To develop the capacity to recognize the beliefs that make up your definition of success, write down five to ten recent actions and ask, "What beliefs led to this action's being chosen?" Be wary of your natural inclination to define logical reasoning for your actions. There may be many potential beliefs for each action, so it is best to identify several possibilities first, then select the motive you think is most correct. Here is an example of what this exercise might look like:

Behavior	Potential Beliefs
Always comes to meetings on time	• Professionals show up to meetings on time. • It is important to respect the time of others. • I am expected to be on time. • If I am late, I will miss something.

»»

Behavior	Potential Beliefs (continued)
Always late to meetings	• Everyone is always late. • It is not important to be on time. • My timetable is more important. • I will not miss anything; this is not worthwhile. • Nobody cares if I am late. • I am too busy to be on time.
Defensive when being given feedback	• I need to prove that I am right. • People who are weak need input and help. • I look bad when others challenge my ideas. • I need to win to feel good. • I do not value the other person's input. • I am embarrassed when challenged in public.
Micromanages	• I am expected to stay on top of what my employees are doing. • If I do not check up on them, they will not complete the work to my satisfaction. • My employees cannot be trusted. • My employees constantly need my help. • This is what good management looks like. • I would rather work with my employees doing these tasks than spend time doing other tasks.
Does not share input in meetings when the agenda is known ahead of time	• I prefer to think things through before commenting. • If someone wants my opinion, he or she will ask me. • I do not want to stick my neck out by sharing my ideas. • This is not my meeting, I am not the leader. • I am not expected to contribute in this meeting.
Regularly discusses ideas and issues with manager	• I am expected to form and share ideas and issues. • My manager wants to hear from me. • I need to make sure my manager knows about the key issues within my area. • Managers should toot their own horn to get noticed.

>>>

Behavior	Potential Beliefs (continued)
Communicates with manager when asked and only on topics asked about	• When it comes to my manager, no news is good news. • Managing on my own is a sign of strength; if I ask my manager to review what's going on, this shows that I am weak and need his or her help. • My manager is too busy to talk to me. I am not a priority.
Avoids counseling others	• If I talk to her, it will make things worse between us. • The discomfort of the conversation will outweigh any benefits. • She will come around on her own. • I have too many tasks to do that are more important. • I don't want to do this.
Does not hesitate to tackle tough personnel issues or to deal with poor performers	• It is my responsibility to handle this issue—it cannot wait. • Performance can only improve if it is dealt with. • If I say nothing, she will more likely fail in the end. • I am accountable for ensuring that everyone performs; there can be no deadweight on the team.

People who are always late to meetings may not consciously think, "My time is more important," but there is a belief that is making being late an acceptable action. To change the behavior, a new belief needs to take its place, such as, "I am expected to be on time" or "being on time shows respect for my peers."

H.I.M.M. Thinking about Success

How do high impact middle managers define success? Each middle manager is going to hold beliefs specific to his or her function and current goals, as those elements are unique. Many aspects of middle management, however, are similar across industries. When observing and talking with high impact middle managers, it becomes apparent that they share similar beliefs about what success means and how it can best be achieved. What's more, these same beliefs are often held by successful senior executives. That is important to note because a senior manager's expectations of his or her middle managers will tend to reflect his or her own beliefs about how success is achieved. An additional benefit of H.I.M.M. thinking is that it will serve middle managers well throughout their career progression. High impact middle managers subscribe to the following beliefs.

Middle managers are expected to be accountable and take ownership—H.I.M.M. is built on the philosophy that in order to achieve results, middle managers need to take ownership for whatever needs to be done. This belief drives proactivity and helps to stave off procrastination.

Middle managers are expected to make a positive contribution to the business—A middle manager's job is to think creatively and proactively, and take initiative to improve his and his team's performance. This belief reinforces the concept that it is *not* a middle manager's job to maintain or oversee what would otherwise happen on its own.

Middle managers should be outstanding role models because they influence the culture and tone of the business—It is not okay for middle managers to be unprofessional or model undesirable behaviors. You will enjoy more success as a manager if you take your role as a professional seriously and recognize that your team members and peers are watching and emulate you when they decide how they should respond to situations.

Middle managers need to get results—Middle managers who believe that it is their job to execute work and deliver results are more likely to choose results-oriented responses and actions. They are also more apt to value productivity measurements and process improvements as tools to monitor, manage, and enhance results.

Management is a social as well as a business function—With every meeting you attend and every conversation you take part in, there is an opportunity to either add to or detract from the quality of the relationship. Middle managers need the support and cooperation of those they work with. Operating in isolation will not yield success. Recognizing that fact will help you choose responses that preserve and build relationships rather than those that destroy communication.

Flexible and nimble teams are more successful—Middle managers must have their finger on the pulse of the company and know when changes in approach make sense and would be of benefit. A manager who holds this belief is more open to exploring options and creative solutions and is less likely to become comfortable with the status quo.

Being a middle manager is a key role—Middle managers should want to spend most of their time managing and facilitating the work of others. Middle managers who do not believe their job is interesting and desirable will not likely serve themselves, or their organization, well.

Success means delivering results and managing people for optimal productivity and satisfaction—In order to be truly effective as a high impact middle manager, you must reframe your definition of success. Success should be defined more by accomplishment and less by promotions, status, or other extrinsically motivating factors such as cash bonuses.

Good managers are responsive to others' ideas and concerns—Being defensive or combative does not reflect favorably on any manager. Being open and flexible makes one seem more intelligent and talented. If you have the constant need to prove that you are right, you will undermine relationships with your superiors and your subordinates.

This list of H.I.M.M. beliefs forms a powerful definition of success! However, you will naturally adopt beliefs specific to challenges you are facing. For example, if over the next year the focus needs to be on product development, you would adopt beliefs and create a vision about how to best manage product development and what outstanding product development looks like.

Imagine what a workplace would look and feel like if all middle managers took on this H.I.M.M. definition of success. The atmosphere would be electric, exciting, and highly productive. What a great place to work! Here's the amazing part: You can adopt these beliefs right now and they will begin to work immediately. To make the H.I.M.M. definition of success a part of your daily management regimen, you should review the beliefs listed on the previous pages and create a list of supporting actions you can take today. Do this daily until the practice has become second nature. The H.I.M.M. Definition of Success Cheat Sheet and Scorecard referenced in the Appendix will also help you incorporate this definition of success into your daily regimen. Incorporating these beliefs into daily and weekly planning will help foster responses that will improve results. For some middle managers, the changes may be so striking that they experience a breakthrough.

Discard Definitions of Success That Produce Failure

In addition to adopting new beliefs that support goals, you may need to discard old beliefs that are not useful or not serving you well. How do you know if your definition of success is constructive? The following questions can help diagnose whether your current beliefs are helpful or harmful:

1 > Are results coming in as expected? If not, why not? What beliefs might be responsible for this shortfall?

2 > On average, how much time is spent being reactive versus proactive? If more time is spent being reactive, why? What beliefs support a focus on reactivity?

3 ❯ Have tasks been pushed aside, delayed, or ignored? If yes, why? What's driving this procrastination?

4 ❯ Does feedback or criticism result in a defensive comeback, shutdown of communication, or combative posture? Why is it important to you to be right or win?

5 ❯ Who in the organization is the most positive and powerful role model? What does he or she do that is so effective? Which beliefs would support these behaviors?

6 ❯ Are team members satisfied with their jobs? Are they frustrated or burned out? If they are frustrated or burned out, why is this and what is the manager's role in fixing this?

7 ❯ How enjoyable is middle management? If it is not satisfying work, why not? Are there new beliefs that can be adopted to improve job satisfaction and impact on the company?

Based on your answers to these questions, you can begin to recognize unhelpful beliefs and redesign your definitions of success. Nonproductive beliefs also become apparent by examining disappointments as they occur. For example, if a project did not go well, do a postmortem to discover why this was the case and to understand the thinking that allowed the failure to occur. Was it a lack of follow-up? Too little research before implementation? Whatever the reasons were, the actions that were taken came from supporting beliefs. Did you assume that everyone would do his or her work on time and that follow-up should not be required? Did you believe that the key vendor had done the research and that nothing would likely go wrong? What if you had taken on the belief that frequent follow-up meetings would be helpful in keeping everyone on track and uncovering areas where the project could get derailed? Would the results have been any different? Yes, they certainly would have.

Besides the H.I.M.M. definition of success previously presented, you, as a middle manager, can define the beliefs that will best serve your goals by completing the following exercise:

- Create a list of management goals for the coming year. These goals should spell out important accomplishments, key initiatives, and areas that will need special managerial attention.
- For each of these goals, identify beliefs that would support success. In other words, what mindset is going to best facilitate goal attainment?

As Ralph Stayer wrote in *Flight of the Buffalo,* "I understand that I am the problem. Accepting that enables me to be the solution." Middle managers who align their beliefs to support their goals will enjoy more success and greater accomplishment. The H.I.M.M. definition of success provides middle managers with a way of thinking about their jobs that is invigorating and dynamic, and that delivers results. This, coupled with beliefs that support specific goals, establishes a winning foundation for any middle manager's journey toward success.

High impact middle managers pay attention to how well their definition of success is serving them. They know that there is a strong link between beliefs, actions, and results. These successful managers have learned that in order to improve results, beliefs that are more effective may need to be adopted while other, less effective beliefs need to be discarded. H.I.M.M. thinking is a distillation of powerful beliefs that can help busy middle managers excel and enjoy their work.

Chapter 3

H.I.M.M. Power Partnership

CLARK WAS A SUCCESSFUL and influential vice president of
human resources. His peers and other senior managers
valued his input and participation. They involved Clark
and his department managers in the day-to-day operations
of their respective departments. Clark's HR department
was effective and well respected to a degree rarely found
in most companies. Because of the fantastic partnership
between Clark's staff and other departments within the
organization, Clark and his team made a positive impact
on the company. However, it wasn't just a one-way street—
other departments influenced Clark and his team as well.
Clark was a powerful role model who demonstrated how
internal departments should collaborate to service each
other and achieve results. Clark also reinforced this belief
in collaboration when it came time to promote and evaluate his team members. Other divisions regularly sought
out candidates from Clark's department, and Clark frequently championed his staff for internal promotions and
other positions within the company.

What made Clark's collaborative approach even more impressive was the fact that his company had a very competitive environment. Department leaders were more inclined to exclude, rather than include, members of internal service teams, like HR. Had it not been for the foundation of partnership that Clark established, other vice presidents in the company would not have given the HR department the same level of consideration or included it in as many initiatives.

Lonny could have learned a few things from Clark. He took credit for work performed by others on his team, to make it appear that he was the one who dreamed up the idea. In meetings, he was a yes-man, always agreeing with higher-level managers to get their nod of approval. Lonny applied for two promotions for which he was technically qualified, but he was turned down for both of them. The fact was that other managers did not feel they could trust Lonny or that he shared their goals. They feared that his personal drive for self-promotion would overshadow the needs of his team and those of the company.

Teamwork Drives Accomplishment

Everyone wants recognition and validation. Evening news programs love to feature stories of heroes who save the day. In the business world, however, the best and most effective way to achieve results is through teamwork—especially at the middle-management level. A group of talented people rallying behind a single cause creates more success than a lone individual going off on his or her own. Middle managers who are good at collaborating are significantly more successful than those who try to go it alone. Clark understood this and was successful. Lonny did not and suffered the consequences professionally.

Developing and maintaining productive partnerships is an important skill for any manager—but most particularly for the high impact middle manager. Why? Because unlike senior executives who give directives, middle managers, more often than not, do not have unilateral decision-making authority. Effective partnerships are a middle manager's currency for getting the work done.

In most companies, departments are interdependent. When things go well, it is rarely because of a single department. It takes many teams, firing on all cylinders, to produce the best results. Middle managers can facilitate their teams' success by working together. By collaborating to improve the performance levels of other teams, middle managers can improve the productivity of their own area.

Middle managers need the cooperation and support of their peers when opportunity knocks or problems occur. Middle managers who take the time to gain peer support for new ideas and initiatives will find that implementation is easier and more trouble-free. Effective high impact middle managers know that their peers are a rich source of ideas and new approaches.

Partners also warn each other about emerging problems and lend a hand in averting a crisis. Communication happens on many levels in most organizations. Some topics are reviewed and discussed in staff meetings. Other information gets sent to employees via e-mail. Sanitized and spun messages are presented to the public. Then there is the dialogue that occurs during informal conversations and lunchtime chats. This last type of information, the informal and unwritten communication, is very important. Emerging concerns, pending decisions, potentially troublesome rumors, and fresh new ideas are most likely to be heard in these outlets first. Middle managers need to develop and maintain excellent relationships with their peers and managers to ensure they are part of this communication pipeline. Working well with other managers also makes work more meaningful and satisfying. When a management team works together, the pace of work quickens and the energy is more positive and oriented toward success. Even when faced with significant challenges, a strong and collaborative management team can make the challenge about finding a creative solution and not about the "problem."

The Traits of Partnership

Effective partnership helps organizations deal with tough challenges and times of growth and opportunity. Partnership goes beyond cooperation to being a purposeful act of inclusion, collaboration, and comanagement. Merely being helpful when solicited or asked does not make one an effective partner. Partners seek each other out and proactively involve each other in day-to-day management conversations and decisions. Effective partnership emerges from a combination of several traits:

Shared purpose

Partners, by definition, are linked to one another. In the business world, partners need to have a sense that they are striving for the same goal. When middle managers have a shared goal, their work together has purpose and meaning. A common goal provides a foundation for partnership. Their opinions and perspectives may differ significantly, but if they are all reaching for the same target, they can find common ground. To create a shared purpose, spend time with other middle managers learning about and discussing each other's goals and challenges.

Shared ownership

When two or more managers share ownership of a result or outcome, they are more likely to work together effectively. Co-owning an outcome takes partnership a step beyond cooperation to collaboration. Senior managers who instill a sense of shared owner-ship among their middle managers will find that this expectation helps drive middle managers to partner with peers, other depart-ments, and clients more often and more effectively. You should have periodic conversations with your peers to clarify roles and expecta-tions in areas of shared ownership. Maintaining an open and posi-tive dialogue will help both of you ensure that your respective areas are optimally managed to produce results.

Mutual trust

Middle managers who trust each another will partner together more effectively. Managers do not need to agree or see things iden-tically to develop trusting and respectful relationships. Often, an appreciation of diverse thoughts and ideas improves the regard managers have for one another. Middle managers who collabo-rate well almost always share mutual trust. Trust is built through the process of active and healthy collaboration and comanagement. By practicing the High Impact Power Partnership techniques that follow, middle managers will begin to build a history together that will enhance trust and openness.

Critical thinking

Without critical thinking, partnership is just small talk. The essence of collaboration is the act of solving problems and gener-ating new ideas together. This work occurs best when all parties are mentally stimulated, productive, and encouraged to think criti-cally. Results are built on the mental capabilities of middle managers working together. High impact middle managers engage their peers in provocative and useful dialogue. Ask open-ended questions and seek ideas for addressing business problems.

Shared success and failure

Middle managers build stronger partnerships when they share the experience of winning and losing. There is nothing like seeing a project through to completion as a team. If the project is a success, celebrating together reinforces the positives of collaboration. When failures occur, middle managers should huddle together to turn the loss into a win. Sharing successes and failures brings the cycle of partnership full circle.

Effective inclusion and communication

Partners talk to each other often and take the initiative to include each other in formative planning and brainstorming conversations. Just as the middle manager should feel a sense of responsibility about communicating effectively with his or her employees, high impact middle managers should expect to keep their fellow middle managers in the loop.

The traits of partnership outlined here describe what peer-to-peer collaboration looks like in action. How do you know if you have been a good partner? You can ask a trusted friend or colleague, although the answer will generally be more favorable than objective. You can also ask your manager, but again, he or she may find it difficult to share concerns and criticisms openly. A better strategy is to read organizational clues. High impact middle managers should observe how other managers interact with each other and compare this to their own experience. Middle managers can also gauge the type of partner they have been by looking at informal communication practices. How often do your peers stop by and ask for input? How open and lively are conversations with colleagues? Look for examples of successes and failures that illustrate good or poor partnership practices. By asking questions of your peers, managers, and coworkers and then watching how they respond and interact, you can begin to glean insight into the type of partner you have been.

H.I.M.M. Power Partnership Techniques

High impact middle managers have learned what it takes to be a great partner. They know that the benefits of effective collaboration far outweigh the time and effort expended in creating the partnership. They also know that good partnerships do not simply happen. There are practices that they must put into place and cultivate to increase the benefits of peer-to-peer collaboration.

Technique #1: Resist the need to control.

If you have a constant need to control situations, people, or conversations, it will undermine effective collaboration with your peer group. Partnering is a give-and-take process in which no one gets to play boss. Listen and watch for verbal and nonverbal clues that suggest other people are feeling pressured or pushed. One of the best ways to give up control in a conversation is to ask more open-ended questions and make fewer opinionated statements.

Technique #2: Spend time with peers.

Management is a social act. The more time that middle managers spend working with one another, the easier and more natural the partnering process will feel. In addition, peers who get together often feel more comfortable asking for input, help, and participation than do those who avoid each other. Middle managers who engage peers only when needed will receive a cooler and less helpful response. Great middle managers, both extroverts and introverts, know the value of cultivating and building relationships.

Technique #3: Resolve any past partnership failures.

Old conflicts and arguments affect the way in which people relate to one another in the present and future. You need to take the initiative to resolve any prior relationship issues in order to pave the way for better and more productive collaboration in the future. The benefits of working through and getting past prior problems with other managers will more than make up for the initial discomfort of broaching the topic with them. Managers who resolve their differences will also feel less work-related stress.

If you are faced with a peer who does not seem willing to improve the relationship, you can do one of three things. First, you might try a different approach. Can you look at the situation from his or her perspective? Have you isolated the key issues or problems? It may be that what you thought was the problem is not what is actually bothering this person. Second, you are the only person you can control. Even if your peer is hanging on to a grudge, make sure that you continue to act and relate in a manner that is professional and collaborative. If you continue to take the high road, he or she might come around in time. Your third option, and the most dramatic, is to work with others whenever possible. You may still need to conduct business with this person, but when given the choice, it is most productive to work with those who reciprocate.

Technique #4: Communicate on behalf of your peers.

Effective communication is one of the most reliable predictors of a healthy partnership. Managers who keep one another in the loop and represent one another well in meetings and other conversations are generally great partners. Communicating with peers should be a regular part of your day. In addition to communicating well with each other, it is important for peers to communicate well on each other's behalf. High impact middle managers are willing and able to represent a peer's interests and needs when that person is not present in staff meetings, brainstorming sessions, and informal conversations. You may need to defend a peer's budget choices, remind others of his or her projects that will require resources, or, more commonly, represent his or her opinions and concerns. Great partners do this even when they do not agree with their peer's point of view. When you represent your peer middle managers in a positive light, you communicate that respect and care for colleagues is a key organizational value.

Technique #5: If you cannot say anything nice, do not say anything at all.

Never badmouth peers in front of others. It never pays to talk badly about peers, and it will burn bridges that you will need later on. Speak respectfully about other managers, even if you think ill of them. Managers who talk about other people behind their backs end up looking bad themselves. It is immature, unprofessional, and destructive to badmouth peers. The saying "What goes around, comes around" certainly applies to workplace relationships. This is not to say that disagreements with peers should be ignored. The best way to deal with a difference of opinion or disagreement is to directly communicate it, in a productive way, to the person involved.

Technique #6: Take ownership of problems and challenges.

Don't pass the buck. Few situations can put a damper on a partnership faster than being hung out to dry by a peer. Catherine learned this the hard way. Harry blamed her for problems that were rooted in his organization. When the president confronted Catherine about this, she was unfairly put on the defensive. Harry's choice to pass blame and abdicate his own involvement in the problem hurt the level of partnership that he and Catherine would have in the future. High impact middle managers own problems and concerns and do not shift the blame onto other managers. If you have a complaint about how another manager is handling a situation, speak to that manager directly before taking it to the next level of management or that individual's boss. You could burn bridges not only with your peer but with upper management as well. If you do need to communicate an issue with another manager, then present a fair and balanced view of the problem, including the part of it that you own.

Technique #7: Graciously share credit.

Partners know that successes come from collaboration and that all players should share the credit. While it may be true that one person's idea was the catalyst for the breakthrough, the overall success was a product of the joint effort. Middle managers who ensure that everyone feels a part of the success will enjoy a positive momentum going into the next project or initiative.

Technique #8: Know the needs and concerns of peers, managers, customers, and employees.

Middle managers will find it is easier to be good partners when they understand the needs and motivations of those with whom they regularly work. They are in a position to anticipate needs, warn of emerging problems, and share ideas with peers if they know what is important to others. As a middle manager, you should be able to answer the following questions regarding your employees and other managers you work with on a daily basis:

- What are their needs? What are their goals? What is their purpose in the organization?
- What are their interests? What are their motivations? (These are often different from their needs.)
- What are their strengths and weaknesses? What unique skills and talents do they bring to the organization?
- What are their hot buttons? What frustrates them most?
- How do they react to change?
- What do I expect from them? What do they expect from me and my department?

CASE STUDY

John and Barry were vice presidents reporting to the division president. They were both very talented and opinionated. When they were together in meetings, their demeanor toward each other was either cool and aloof or confrontational. The real problem, however, came when they were not together. Both John and Barry took cheap shots at each other's expense in front of others. They also did not involve each other in decisions as often as they should have, preferring to avoid each other when possible. Barry was particularly critical and cynical of John and many of his group members. Neither were inexperienced middle managers; they should have known better than to relate in this dysfunctional way. However, even managers with decades of experience let their opinions and emotions get the best of them. The managers who reported to John and Barry were beginning to emulate the dysfunction between the groups. It took having a manager who worked for John and closely with Barry to call their attention to what was going on. To their credit, once they saw the impact their poor relationship had on their results and their teams, they were able to become effective partners. In just a couple of months, the improvement was significant and both were realizing benefits in terms of productivity and work satisfaction.

Middle managers who practice the eight partnering techniques will see immediate and long-term benefits. When peers become advocates and coaches, they add value to your quest for results and efficiency. Being a good partner will also reflect well on you and improve your promotability and value within the organization.

Effective partnerships are valuable assets for managers. Developing and maintaining productive relationships with peers, managers, and team members allows high impact middle managers to extend their reach into the organization and improve their effectiveness. Great partners share ownership of projects and work together to enjoy success and recover from failure. H.I.M.M. Power Partnership techniques such as spending more time with peers, resolving relationship issues, and representing others well can help middle managers improve peer relationships.

Part Two

**Planning for Execution—
A Must for H.I.M.M. Leaders**

Chapter 4

The H.I.M.M. Reality Check — Measuring Current Performance

UNTIL HIS LAST DAY OF WORK, Tom would have said that his performance was meeting the expectations of his manager. Unfortunately, he was dead wrong. Tom was a poor manager and his boss felt that Tom and his team did not produce satisfactory work. Tom was not an effective communicator and others felt he was untrustworthy. Tom's manager had asked for changes that Tom neither implemented nor delegated to the team—even though he told his manager he would. Several conversations occurred between Tom and his manager, but Tom was never able to grasp where things stood or how his manager viewed his performance.

When people in the home office spoke about Tom's colleague, Ron, their eyes would roll and they would exchange a familiar look of, "Oh, that guy." Senior managers felt that Ron was a marginal manager, someone they would replace if they could find a better alternative. Unfortunately, he had specialized technical skills that made him hard to replace. Ron openly disparaged the company, as well as its policies and procedures. He seemed to take pride in being disrespectful and insubordinate in front of his employees. In addition, his lack of professionalism and negative demeanor rubbed off on others. A highly respected manager became a marginally performing employee after working only a few short months under Ron's supervision. Turnover on Ron's team was high. What was perhaps most unbelievable was the fact that even though he was open and brash with his opinions and criticisms, Ron had no idea that the senior management team held him in such low regard.

Jane, on the other hand, preferred to see the bright side of every story. Her glass was always half full. While this perspective served her well in many situations, when it came to her job, her Pollyanna take on things became her undoing. She managed a department that produced several major projects each year, but Jane could not get the work done on time or in an organized fashion. Jane's manager had several specific conversations about areas where Jane needed to improve. But Jane did not internalize the feedback and correct her performance. She chose, instead, to believe that as long as she worked hard, everything would be fine. "I'm doing the best I can" became a frequent response when her manager asked questions about late projects. Jane was in denial.

Unlike Tom, Ron, or Jane, Bob was smart, creative, and a great asset to the company. Yet he had no idea that several senior managers thought he was one of the more important managers on the team. Bob knew that he was doing okay but did not feel the satisfaction and acknowledgment equal to his managers' opinion of his performance. When times were tough and the organization needed to reduce staff, Bob worried that he would be first on the list of expendable managers. In reality, he was on the list of managers too important to let go.

Tom, Ron, Jane, and Bob all suffered from a poor or inaccurate definition of how their managers and the organization viewed their performance. Unfortunately, this is a common problem that gets in the way of a middle manager's ability to be successful. The reason this was the case may be obvious with Tom, Ron, or Jane because their performance was unsatisfactory and their careers were in jeopardy. But Bob's inaccurate perception about his performance also affected his success even though he underestimated his value and worth to the organization.

When you, as a middle manager, are unaware or unclear about current performance levels, it is more difficult for you to set appropriate goals and targets. Efforts for improvement need to begin with a benchmark and include a plan for transitioning from today's reality to tomorrow's goal. Middle managers can significantly improve their results when they understand:

- How their managers would evaluate their performance
- The reputation they have in their organization
- How well their teams are meeting goals and producing results
- How the organization perceives their teams' contributions and effectiveness

Most middle managers do not have an understanding of all these areas because open, candid, and helpful feedback is not the norm in most organizations. This is a shame because knowing current performance is instrumental to most change and improvement plans. Many change efforts fail because they do not consider and incorporate today's realities. Ignorance is definitely not bliss when it comes to managing people, projects, and processes.

For middle managers to produce the best results possible, all goals and plans need to recognize and consider current levels of performance. It is critical that you know how your superiors, peers, and employees view your performance. By establishing the right benchmark, or starting point, improvement plans will be more realistic and operational.

The H.I.M.M. reality check is a set of techniques that you can use to understand your own performance level and the current effectiveness of your team. These techniques include methods for:

- Assessing your reputation within the organization
- Assessing your team's reputation within the organization
- Measuring your team's performance against goals and results
- Communicating current performance findings to your managers and team members

High impact middle managers have a strong self-awareness and know how to keep their ear to the ground to listen for valuable information about how they and their teams are doing. The journey from good to great, or great to greater, is paved with well-planned initiatives and improvement efforts. High impact middle managers have learned that successfully planned and implemented improvement initiatives start with good information.

How to Assess Your Reputation Within the Organization

Middle managers must understand the reputation they have in their organization, be it positive or not as good as they would like. Peers, managers, and team members respond differently to each middle manager based on past results and how that manager has reacted in good times and bad. The quality of relationships plays a big part in determining a manager's reputation. Middle managers with poor reputations will find it harder to garner support for initiatives and will likely not receive full and helpful collaborative efforts from others. When people say that a manager has a good reputation, they are saying that he or she:

Can be trusted—Managers are perceived as trustworthy when their words and actions are consistent. Trustworthiness is also impacted by a middle manager's ability to keep confidences and represent others in a positive and professional way. Being caught talking about someone behind his or her back is a quick way to become known as untrustworthy.

Does what he or she promises—Keeping promises means doing what was agreed to, whether the agreement was spoken, written, or implied. Fulfilling implied agreements is just as important as keeping promises etched in stone or e-mail. Middle managers who follow through on the commitments they make have integrity and will enjoy greater respect than managers who routinely do not deliver on their commitments.

Produces good results—Middle managers who pull their weight and add value to the company are respected and appreciated. Delivering results is a fundamental requirement of all middle managers. Managers who produce poor results will not be well regarded by other managers or peers because they are not doing their part to contribute to corporate success. The exception to this is if the results are lacking due to conditions not in the middle manager's control.

Is pleasurable or easy to work with—Managers who other staff members like to work with will be perceived more favorably than those who are less fun and amiable. It is not important that a manager be an extrovert in order for him or her to be considered a pleasure to work with. Managers of all styles and philosophical persuasions can be easy to work with as long as they are accessible, interested, and helpful.

Is knowledgeable and creative in his or her chosen field—Managers and peers acknowledge and appreciate middle managers who know their stuff. This includes technical or specialized skills related to the department they manage. Furthermore, others in the organization will think well of middle managers who continue to learn and grow.

Is an asset to the company—In most companies only a small percentage of middle managers are outstanding assets to the company. When senior management considers a middle manager to be a great asset, that middle manager is someone who has demonstrated the ability and desire to contribute to the organization in a variety of ways. He or she tends to be a manager who could successfully manage most departments or projects.

When a manager has a bad reputation, people think that he or she:

Cannot be trusted—Perhaps he or she has abused confidences or burned someone in the past?

Does not follow through on commitments—Has he or she let people down?

Does not get the job done when others do—Are his or her results disappointing?

Is in some way difficult to work with—Is he or she not a team player?

Does not have the right skills or aptitude—Does he or she lack creativity or technical expertise?

Is not an important contributor—Does he or she make any difference?

You probably will find it difficult and uncomfortable to take the steps necessary to learn about the reputation you have established in your organization. However, it should be even more undesirable to have no idea how others perceive you.

Middle managers can use one or more of the following three approaches to discover their reputation. The first, and easiest, approach is to ask. This method will work in environments where honest and open feedback is available. Middle managers should also try the second approach, which is observation, particularly if the first approach does not yield full or truthful information. Many peers, managers, and team members will not feel comfortable being candid with their thoughts. If the first two approaches fail to provide you with the necessary information, then try the third approach, which is to use an objective third party. Managers who need to use the third approach will often have a reputation that makes people reluctant and guarded with their feedback. In addition, middle managers in higher-level positions receive less honest feedback than their colleagues at lower levels do. Some people will be reluctant, for example, to tell a vice president about areas in which he or she needs to improve. Middle managers should be aware that it is going to be harder to get useful and helpful feedback as they progress up the ladder in their organization. This is unfortunate, because everyone needs good feedback to perform at his or her best.

Approach #1: Ask.

An effective way for you to determine your reputation is to ask peers, managers, and team members. This, of course, works best if you have a trusting and collaborative relationship that allows for open and honest communication. The questions that you ask and the way in which you ask them are also important. A sample form you can use to solicit feedback is on the following pages.

Ask your peers, managers, and team members to fill out this form and return it. You can choose to have the form returned directly to you or to another person if you think this will help people be more open and honest. Ask for a response within five days and encourage respondents to be open and honest. Compile the responses. Notice the trends and the relative rankings. While respondents may not feel comfortable answering questions in a derogatory manner, the

Middle Management Survey for: _____

Please answer the survey openly and honestly. I am interested in learning the good, the bad, and the ugly. I consider this tool to be a part of my overall development plan and value your feedback. Please return the completed survey to _____ by _____. Thank you!

Part 1: Middle Management Qualities and Traits

For each trait listed, indicate whether this particular trait is a strength of mine or a weakness or somewhere in the middle. If a weakness, please do not hesitate to point this out. Please also rank these traits from 1 to 7, 1 being the trait I am strongest in and 7 the trait that is my greatest weakness.

MIDDLE MANAGEMENT QUALITY/TRAIT	STRENGTH	AVERAGE	WEAKNESS	RANK
Timeliness of work and projects				
Reliability				
Easy to work with, even when times are difficult				
Acts quickly and follows up				
Results orientation				
Skilled manager				
Builds and maintains relationships				

Middle Management Survey *(continued)*

Part 2: Open-Ended Questions

Please complete the following questions providing as many specifics as possible.

Share a time when this manager let someone down at work.

Share the most important contribution this manager has made to the business in the past year.

What has been his or her greatest failure in the past year?

How well do you believe this manager represents you and your interests?

Do you consider this manager highly productive, satisfactorily productive, or below average in productivity?

What do people like most and least about working with this manager?

Most:

Least:

Middle Management Survey *(continued)*

Part 3: Descriptive Phrases

Each section below contains four phrases. Spread 100 points across the four phrases, giving more points to those phrases that are more descriptive of this manager and his or her performance and fewer points to those phrases that are less descriptive. You can, for example, give 50 points to the first two phrases and 0 points to the other two, or give 30 points to one while giving the others 20, 10, and 40 points, respectively.

MANAGEMENT STYLE	100 POINTS TOTAL
Teamwork oriented	
Values individual initiative and creativity	
Values security and predictability	
Hard-driving competitiveness and focus on results	

THIS MANAGER IS THOUGHT TO BE	100 POINTS TOTAL
Trustworthy	
Reliable	
A good partner	
Responsible	

WHEN TIMES GET TOUGH/BUSY, THIS MANAGER	100 POINTS TOTAL
Plans well and is organized	
Can get emotional	
Represents the needs of his or her team members well	
Can get overwhelmed	

ranking and ratings will reveal which of the managerial traits are of the most concern. For example, if a manager is not reliable, chances are good that respondents will rank this trait toward the bottom, or 7, in most of the returned forms.

You may also choose to meet with people one-on-one, but this approach is going to yield accurate results only in the most open and trusting work environments.

To interpret the results: The completed survey on the following pages represents real feedback given to a middle manager. The scores have all been averaged.

The feedback that this particular middle manager should get from this survey is that, overall, he or she is very well regarded and respected by the folks who participated. This group sees him or her as an extremely results-oriented and highly productive manager. These are very positive scores. Even with positive scores such as these, there will likely be one or two areas that need improvement. This middle manager's results are no exception. First, it is clear that developing relationships is a relative weakness for this manager and may even be a potential future derailing factor. Related to this is his or her tendency to judge others and come across as too blunt and direct. These criticisms are all related to how this middle manager works with others. It is also apparent that he or she needs to be more cognizant of how he or she comes across and how he or she talks about other people.

It is likely that this middle manager has been battling these weaknesses throughout his or her career. Without this feedback, it is likely that these problem areas could become more severe and begin affecting his or her career. It is also quite interesting that this middle manager scored no points in part 3 under the option "can get emotional." While this means that he or she keeps her cool, it is also related to his or her tendency to lack empathy and be too matter-of-fact.

As these results show, even very strong and well-respected middle managers will benefit from learning more about the reputation they

Middle Management Survey for: *Ms./Mr. Middle Manager*

Please answer the survey openly and honestly. I am interested in learning the good, the bad, and the ugly. I consider this tool to be a part of my overall development plan and value your feedback. Please return the completed survey to _____ by _____. Thank you!

Part 1: Middle Management Qualities and Traits

For each trait listed, indicate whether this particular trait is a strength of mine or a weakness or somewhere in the middle. If a weakness, please do not hesitate to point this out. Please also rank these traits from 1 to 7, 1 being the trait I am strongest in and 7 the trait that is my greatest weakness.

MIDDLE MANAGEMENT QUALITY/TRAIT	STRENGTH	AVERAGE	WEAKNESS	RANK
Timeliness of work and projects	X,X,X,X,X			4.25
Reliability	X,X,X,X,X			3.75
Easy to work with, even when times are difficult	X,X,X,X	X		4.5
Acts quickly and follows up	X,X,X,X,X,X			3.25
Results orientation	X,X,X,X,X,X			1.25
Skilled manager	X,X,X,X	X		3.5
Builds and maintains relationships	X	X,X,X,X,X		6.75

Middle Management Survey *(continued)*

Part 2: Open-Ended Questions

Please complete the following questions providing as many specifics as possible.

Share a time when this manager let someone down at work.
Too quick to pass judgment. Cannot think of a time. Only minor things (4).
Share the most important contribution this manager has made to the business in the past year.
Department workflow. Developing good processes. Elevated the level of her department (3).
What has been his or her greatest failure in the past year?
Don't know. Qualities of all her employees not up to standard (3).
How well do you believe this manager represents you and your interests?
Very well. Always honest. Well, always supportive. For the most part excellent, but there may also be times when she gives an opinion about me that is inaccurate and is not helpful.
Do you consider this manager highly productive, satisfactorily productive, or below average in productivity?
Highly productive (5).
What do people like most and least about working with this manager?
Most: Knows her stuff. Is always there for you. Thoroughness and dependability. Smart, quick, funny. Gets things done.
Least: Can be very matter-of-fact, lacking empathy. Afraid you may not measure up in her eyes. Blunt. Sometimes abrupt and too direct. Keeps people focused and honest.

Middle Management Survey *(continued)*

Part 3: Descriptive Phrases

Each section below contains four phrases. Spread 100 points across the four phrases, giving more points to those phrases that are more descriptive of this manager and his or her performance and fewer points to those phrases that are less descriptive. You can, for example, give 50 points to the first two phrases and 0 points to the other two, or give 30 points to one while giving the others 20, 10, and 40 points, respectively.

MANAGEMENT STYLE	100 POINTS TOTAL
Teamwork oriented	31
Values individual initiative and creativity	31
Values security and predictability	11
Hard-driving competitiveness and focus on results	27

THIS MANAGER IS THOUGHT TO BE	100 POINTS TOTAL
Trustworthy	28
Reliable	26
A good partner	22
Responsible	24

WHEN TIMES GET TOUGH/BUSY, THIS MANAGER	100 POINTS TOTAL
Plans well and is organized	56
Can get emotional	0
Represents the needs of his or her team members well	44
Can get overwhelmed	0

have developed in the organization. Paying attention to relative rankings and the recurring themes will help you to better understand your strengths and weaknesses.

Approach #2: Observe.

Another way that middle managers can determine their reputation is to observe how others interact with and around them. Peers, managers, and team members will communicate in ways that reflect their feelings. Middle managers should take note of the following:

Inclusivity versus exclusivity—Managers held in high regard will find themselves invited to participate in more conversations and meetings to discuss emerging issues than will middle managers who do not enjoy as positive a reputation.

Project assignments—Highly regarded middle managers will find that senior managers ask them to lead or take part in important projects.

Confidential information—All middle managers are privy to some proprietary company information. There are many conversations, however, that take place about new ideas, potential deals, and upcoming changes in the organization. Managers learn who does not keep confidences or likes to spread gossip. If you find yourself excluded from sensitive information, your reputation may be suffering.

What happens in tough situations—Results-oriented middle managers will be the logical go-to people when something needs to be done quickly and well. Managers who have failed to meet deadlines or produce results in the past will not be on the top of the list of folks to go to when opportunity or problems strike.

Confidence in goals and deadlines—Middle managers known for delivering on their goals and deadlines will find that others have confidence in their work and plans.

Collaboration and cooperation from peers—Peers and managers will treat middle managers who have been great partners more warmly and collaboratively than they do those who have not been good partners. Peers are also more likely to look out for those who have established a positive and strong reputation.

Career progression—Middle managers can get an indication about their reputation by looking at how their career has progressed. This includes promotions they have received as well as those that they wanted but did not receive. Middle managers who fail to receive promotions should assume there is probably something about their reputation that needs improvement.

Feedback and performance evaluations—Middle managers should notice what their manager does and does not say when providing feedback or explaining a performance evaluation. Which skills or responsibilities does the manager, without hesitation, say are the middle manager's strengths? Which responsibilities does the manager talk about using qualifiers or less favorable terms?

Managers who notice how others treat them should be able to get a feel for the reputation they have within the organization. When evaluating reputation, it is important to separate interactions and inclusion initiated because of one's position from other situations. The CFO must provide input on finances, the physicist will take part in projects involving physics, and the captain needs to answer questions about navigation. Senior managers ask their valued middle managers to join in a variety of discussions and projects and include them early-on in situations or problems that occur.

Approach #3: Use a facilitator or third party.

If you do not want to use approaches 1 and 2, or have tried them without success, you might want to enlist help from an objective third party. In many companies, this is a regular and normal practice. Some organizations have a corporate psychologist on staff or executive coaches who help senior and middle managers discover and improve their reputations. Other organizations use human resources (HR) generalists or management-development trainers to meet this need. Depending on the situation, an objective third party can use surveys, interviews, and observation to help you determine how to improve your effectiveness.

Another objective method that many companies use is 360-degree feedback instruments. These surveys are often used and chosen because they collect and compare information from the person (a self-assessment) as well as his or her manager(s), peers, and employees. Most 360-degree instruments have questions that measure the middle manager's reputation. These feedback instruments, however, are only as good as the data that go into them and the follow-up that results from them. They are most useful if you can get several peers, team members, and managers to complete the surveys and then positively and proactively respond to the feedback you receive.

Middle managers interested in learning what their reputations are in an organization can use any of these approaches. Great managers do what others don't or won't. Many managers never bother to think about how others see them or if they have a derailing factor getting in the way of their success. Middle managers who take the time and energy to discover their reputations will experience, at the very least, an "aha" moment and, at best, a breakthrough. High impact middle managers know what their strengths and weaknesses are and use this knowledge to grow and improve.

When faced with a significant derailing factor affecting their career, many managers crumble. High impact middle managers, however, use it as an opportunity to create a new definition of success. They look at what can be improved because they realize that success and accolades will naturally follow as a result of being an

> ## CASE STUDY
>
> Art had applied for two promotions and received neither. The position Art had applied for was an internal support position that would interact with many other departments. When managers from other departments found out that Art had applied for the promotion, several expressed their concerns. They didn't want to work with Art. Though he was highly qualified, Art did not have the most important qualification: demonstrated ability and experience developing and maintaining positive work relationships. The hiring manager told Art the truth. Art was not going to get the position because he had a reputation for being difficult to work with and had burned bridges with internal customers over the past year. Until Art fixed these problems, his career would go nowhere.

outstanding partner to work with. Many managers find that they can repair burned bridges and re-establish credibility by consistently being collaborative and productive. It can be hard to deal with harsh feedback but not doing so can permanently derail your career.

How to Assess Your Team's Reputation Within the Organization

The HR team at ABC company was well regarded and enjoyed high levels of participation in most of the company's major initiatives. Many departments viewed working with HR as a positive and worthwhile activity and felt that the HR team helped them manage their part of the business more effectively. Members of the HR team were proud of their accomplishments and took their role of supporting the organization seriously. Other business units coveted these HR team members for open positions and most team members experienced positive career moves every two years or so.

The accounting department, on the other hand, was known as being inflexible, inaccurate, and slow. Managers did not trust the numbers produced by the department and felt they had to clean up after their errors. The processes the accounting department used and the way they conducted business made it more difficult for managers to manage their departments. Many individuals on the accounting team did not progress or receive promotions. Of the talented employees who joined the team, many left within six months. The employees who stayed on the team were marginal performers. The situation was so bad that people in other departments often circumvented processes in order to avoid contact with the accounting department.

These two examples may seem extreme, but both are real and commonplace. Most middle managers would like to see their team regarded similarly to the HR team in this example and not like the accounting team. By taking the time to evaluate your team's reputation, you will have the information and starting point you need to begin the improvement process. All teams have the potential for being well-regarded high performers. Making sure that your team is making a positive contribution to the organization should be your top priority because it will drive success, satisfaction, and results. To discover and define your team's reputation in the organization, you should:

- Ask peers and managers
- Observe and listen
- Measure performance
- Talk to team members

Ask peers and managers

To assess the reputation of your team, you can ask many of the same questions you would use to determine your own reputation. For individuals or teams alike, reputations form around similar questions: Can they be trusted? Do they deliver results? Are they positive to work with? Are they reliable? Are they responsive? To understand the answers to these questions, middle managers should regularly talk to their peers and managers, asking open-ended questions like these:

- In what ways does this department excel?
- In what ways does this department fail to meet expectations?
- If you were the manager, what improvement or changes would you make to this team?
- What is it like to work with this team?
- When was the last time you felt frustrated because of this team's performance or an interaction with team members?
- What is one change that would make working with this team more pleasurable?
- What do others say about this team?

When a middle manager talks to his or her peers and managers about how to improve team performance, he or she will often get valuable information about how they currently regard the team. Discovering a team's reputation is not as hard as determining one's own reputation.

Observe and listen

Middle managers can also pick up information about their team's reputation by paying attention to verbal and nonverbal clues. In meetings, how do people refer to the team? When project managers assign tasks for a cross-functional project, is the team included begrudgingly or as an important contributor? Do people try to include team members or go around them to get their work done? It is common practice to see alternative systems and processes pop up for the sole purpose of not having to involve a particular department or team. If this happens, it should be a giant clue that your team suffers from a poor reputation. For example, with the accounting team mentioned earlier, several departments tracked their own data and created their own reports. A couple of departments found ways around the purchasing system to get the items they needed on time. Middle managers who make it a point to observe these activities can be more proactive in preventing needless duplication of work and improving their team's performance and reputation.

Measure performance

Teams that meet their goals and produce results will often also have a positive reputation in the organization. Middle managers should know how their team is performing for many reasons, including understanding if the company sees the team as a positive contributor. The next section offers techniques for measuring team performance.

Talk to team members

If the team is enjoying a positive reputation, team members will feel pride and satisfaction. If the team has a poor reputation, this will likely be a source of stress and frustration for team members. For middle managers, there are two advantages to asking team members about the team's reputation. First, managers will learn valuable and useful information that they can use to set goals and select improvement initiatives. Second, team members who talk about their performance are more likely to become part of the solution and improvement effort. As well as asking your team members' opinions, try to solicit input and ideas for getting to the next level of performance.

How to Measure Your Team's Performance Against Goals and Results

Along with understanding your team's reputation, you also need to measure its performance in order to establish the correct goals. This goes beyond knowing that everyone is working hard and doing their best, to taking the time to measure throughput and results.

Often, a team is producing much more than the manager or the organization realizes. Sometimes the reverse is also true. Clearly defining current performance helps establish the starting point for all goals and initiatives. Many managers think of measuring performance as an undesirable and a low-value-added task. How mistaken these managers are! Team performance measures help middle managers gain the support and resources they need and make their job easier and more fruitful. Read the following case study:

CASE STUDY

Tim's predecessors had requested additional personnel to process the massive amounts of information that flowed through his department. Senior managers turned down their requests and, in some cases, cut their resources. Tim could see the need for people to process the information more effectively and quickly and knew that he would need senior managers' support to dedicate resources in this area. Tim did something the managers before him had not. He measured performance and productivity. He determined that each employee spent over 35 percent of his or her time on processing, and that as a team, their efficiency was lower than desired. By dedicating personnel to the processing tasks, efficiency would improve and overall personnel costs would decrease. Had Tim not measured current performance and produced the data to back up his assertions, it is unlikely that he would have found support for creating new positions.

High impact middle managers make it a priority to know and continually measure their team's performance. They do so by establishing ongoing systems and practices for updating and communicating throughput and results. They know the key financial and nonfinancial metrics that matter most. To determine the correct things to measure, ask yourself the following questions:

1 **❯** What is the most important contribution that internal and external customers expect this team to make? Is the team meeting the expectations of internal and external customers?

2 ❯ What are the primary products and services produced by this team? What is its productivity and throughput related to these products and services?

3 ❯ Is the team meeting its goals? Why or why not?

4 ❯ How would this team's internal and external customers define the responsiveness and speed that they expect from this team? Is the team meeting expectations?

5 ❯ What major initiatives or projects is this team supporting? Are team members completing their work on time and well?

6 ❯ What expectations exist about improving departmental processes and methods? Are team members taking time and the initiative to improve how they do their work?

Based on the answers to these questions, you can begin to identify the most important metrics to track. It is helpful to create a quick reference of several metrics, to regularly review with your team members and managers (a tool for communicating metrics, called the H.I.M.M. Playbook, is presented in Chapter 5). Furthermore, middle managers who involve the team in measuring and reporting on these metrics will improve their team members' connection, empowerment, and ownership of the department's results and success.

How to Communicate Current Performance Findings to Managers and Team Members

Some middle managers take the time to measure performance but then fail to communicate performance to their team members or their managers. Management is a social act; if you collect information but do nothing with it, then you are not truly managing. Measurements can be useful only when managers and team members discuss, respond to, and use measurement information to improve

CASE STUDY

Each year during the budgeting process, senior managers challenged Corky to lower the HR department's headcount. This was always a frustrating process because she knew that, if anything, she needed more help. Although the company was small, it hired and then laid off many seasonal employees each year. Corky measured the throughput and results of the HR team. The numbers were enlightening and helpful. The department was recruiting, hiring, processing, evaluating, and terminating employees at a rate more typical of a company four times its size. The usual ratio of 1 HR person for every 100 employees would not work for this department. Corky did need more help and, with good information and measurements, was able to get it.

performance in the future. To communicate current performance, middle managers should:

Meet regularly with their manager to review performance— At this meeting, you should come prepared with a list of current performance measures, a summary of those things that are going well, concerns, and your action plan for addressing the concerns. This meeting can be brief, as short as thirty minutes. Middle managers should meet with their managers on at least a monthly basis. During peak production periods or major initiatives, meetings should occur more often.

Discuss team performance and metrics at every team meeting— Ask open-ended questions to clarify concerns or to collect team members' ideas for resolving issues with throughput or results. Speak about concerns and performance shortfalls in a matter-of-fact way that communicates to team members that performance needs to improve but that this is not something personal.

Post team measurements in a visible way—Ensure the team updates key performance measures regularly. Each team should have three to five fundamental deliverables that are most important.

For example, the human resource team might track hiring accuracy and short-term turnover.

Use information about current performance levels when planning future initiatives or setting goals—Projects and initiatives will be more successful if they account for and consider the team's strengths and weaknesses.

Be sure to celebrate excellent team performance, major milestones, and accomplishments—Share these important performance achievements with peers and the rest of the organization.

Communicating current team performance enables managers and team members to react and begin the process of celebration or improvement. Most middle managers do not talk about team performance enough with their teams or managers. The many rewards of regular and open conversations about metrics include higher manager confidence, improved team morale, and better results.

When you understand the reputation you have in an organization, the reputation of your team, and their current performance metrics, you arm yourself with powerful information that will aid in planning, goal setting, and improvement initiatives. High impact middle managers perform the H.I.M.M. reality check by practicing habits and employing methods that ensure they are aware of their work environment. In time, these habits and methods will become second nature and a normal part of your middle-management practices.

Chapter 5

Using the H.I.M.M. Playbook to Facilitate Peak Performance

IN SPORTS, THE GOALS ARE CLEAR. Well-conceived and clearly communicated plays determine what each player does. Objectives are clarified during practice sessions, and each team member's performance is reviewed in detail after each game. Every player knows his or her stats and those of the team. Skill and results determine each team member's position and play time. Like a great coach, high impact middle managers use planning, measurement, and communication skills to create performance targets and improve team accountability, execution, and results.

Just as a sports team uses a playbook to develop strategy and refine its game plan, so, too, can high impact middle managers use a similar tool to refine their management practices and facilitate peak performance from themselves and their team. Using the H.I.M.M. Playbook will enable you to set goals, establish plans, and measure performance in less time than with more conventional methods. The result will be significant improvements in work completion, quality, and throughput.

The H.I.M.M. Playbook

In sports, teams need to respond quickly and plan well between each game. They do not have time for elaborate processes or cumbersome tracking mechanisms. The H.I.M.M. Playbook uses the efficient and time-saving aspects of the playbooks used in sports and adds features that meet the needs of busy middle managers.

Elements of a typical sports playbook include:

- The strategy for each game
- A list of regular plays organized by category
- Strategies for communicating and exchanging plays with others
- Detailed statistics on each player and the players on the opposing team
- Strengths and weaknesses of the team and its opponents

The H.I.M.M. Playbook contains measures, indicators, and lists that many businesses track and value. It is important that you use this playbook only as a starting point. The playbook will be most useful when middle managers customize it to meet the needs of their departments. Its elements include:

- Descriptions of priorities and approaching projects
- Short-term and long-term goals
- Detailed metrics on the key financial and nonfinancial measures for the team
- Ongoing work productivity statistics

- Space for updates on work projects or tasks
- Ways of optimizing workflow
- A list of concerns and barriers facing the team

The H.I.M.M. Playbook is an invaluable tool that will help you focus your time and energy on the tasks that will have the greatest impact on your team's results. It provides a snapshot of current team performance, priorities, and work assignments. Here is a detailed description of each part of the H.I.M.M. Playbook:

Priorities and approaching projects

This section should include a brief list of future projects or initiatives that team members should consider and begin preparing for when planning their work. For example, if you work in a company that experiences seasonal highs and lows, this section can be used to remind team members of important launch dates for busy times.

Short-term and long-term goals

Short-term goals are those your team will complete in the next one to six months. Long-term goals should mirror or support those listed in the strategic plan. Well-written goals include time frames, owners of tasks, and expected results. Reviewing both short-term and long-term goals on a regular basis helps your team stay aligned and able to meet today's needs and support the company's vision for the future. Other sections of the playbook should include tasks that support the goals listed here.

Key financial and nonfinancial team metrics

Each team should have a set of metrics that it collects, reviews, and reports periodically. These metrics measure how well the team is doing relative to the fundamental contributions they have been asked to make to the company. For a marketing team, for example, the metrics could include customer acquisition costs, return on investments (ROIs) for marketing campaigns, and exposure in the marketplace. If you are not already tracking this type of data, you should start, because this information will help you stay abreast of performance and enable you to notice trends and emerging problems.

Ongoing work productivity

Each department has ongoing work that is important to track. Often this work will consume a significant portion of your team's time and resources. Examples of this type of work include processing checks, answering customer calls, processing new employees, maintaining systems, and supporting field operations. In this section of the H.I.M.M. Playbook, you should list two or three of the most important ongoing products or services and describe how the team will track productivity. The items in this section will probably not change much from week to week, but productivity will vary with time.

Work projects and tasks

This portion of the H.I.M.M. Playbook is the most dynamic and offers the clearest and quickest benefit to middle managers. Tasks that your team needs to complete are listed with deadlines and owners for each task. As your team completes tasks, you can take these tasks off the playbook or leave them listed to help team members communicate the status of their work. Some managers will prefer to complete one playbook each week and keep previous copies in their day planner. Others may choose to keep one master playbook.

Workflow optimization

Middle managers use the H.I.M.M. Playbook to track work against current and emerging priorities. By reviewing the playbook often and asking yourself questions about how you are using your resources, you can ensure that your team is producing at its best. Middle managers should also recognize and plan for short periods of high or low work demands by adjusting assignments or bringing in short-term help.

Concerns and barriers

Listing concerns and barriers is critical to keeping you and your team members focused on resolving problems that could affect throughput. Throughout the day and week, the middle manager fills this section with the normal challenges of running a business. As he or she crosses each entry off the list, it is a sign that work is flowing productively again. This section, more than any other, highlights high impact middle management work in action!

Communicating the Playbook

Sports teams use their playbooks faithfully. It is the central tool for communicating priorities and progress to the team. Producing consistent wins takes team-wide communication and participation.

This approach is not as common in business—though it should be. During Black & Decker's DeWalt line development and launch, product teams met frequently to discuss status, priorities, and their game plan. They also took time to celebrate successes along the way. Sometimes the team congratulated the engineers for creating a new and better feature. Other times, the marketing folks won praise for a well-timed coup in the marketplace.

Middle managers in any industry can use the H.I.M.M. Playbook in the same manner. Management is a social act and the H.I.M.M. Playbook is an excellent way to facilitate communication between you and your supervisors, team members, peers, and manager. The H.I.M.M. Playbook is an organic tool, which should change to represent the current priorities and needs of your department. Middle managers should have their H.I.M.M. Playbook with them at all meetings and review it at the beginning of each workday. Those who use a day planner for appointments should insert their playbook into their binder for easy reference. High-tech middle managers who prefer PDAs or laptops can load their H.I.M.M. Playbook into their favorite device. By reviewing each section of the Playbook at team meetings, middle managers can get input from team members on items to change or add, as well as gain understanding and commitment for the priorities. This practice will also provide an opportunity for team members to ask questions, express concerns, identify barriers, and ask for necessary support.

How to Use the H.I.M.M. Playbook

You can begin using the H.I.M.M. Playbook by filling out each section and sharing it with your managers and team members for input. If you do not currently have team metrics, you can take a few minutes to think about what they should be or hold a team meeting to

H.I.M.M. Playbook

Ongoing Work	Status	Key Metrics	Current Performance	Priorities and Upcoming Projects
			Concerns and Barriers!

Short-Term Goals		Long-Term Goals		

H.I.M.M. Playbook (continued)

Task	Owner	Deadline	Task	Owner	Deadline

Productivity Questions
Why are we doing this?
What difference will it make?
Is there a better action to take?
Is there an easier way?
Are the right people involved?
Does it improve results?

discuss metrics as a group. Long- and short-term goals come from yearly plans. Middle managers who are not presently creating a departmental plan can use the tutorial at the end of this chapter.

Update the playbook daily, weekly, or as needed. Take it to all meetings. Information shared at meetings often fits into the Upcoming Projects or Concerns and Barriers sections. You will want to keep these and other sections current to get the most benefit from using the H.I.M.M. Playbook.

Use the H.I.M.M. Playbook as a platform for team update meetings. Revise and redistribute copies after each meeting so all of your team members understand the plan and the action items they are responsible for. Share the H.I.M.M. Playbook with the peers who work most closely with your team. Doing so will create greater understanding, generate support, and improve relationships. The H.I.M.M. Playbook is an excellent communication tool.

Middle managers can download the H.I.M.M. Playbook in various sizes and file formats at *www.haneberg-management.com.* Follow the High Impact Middle Management links. Finding a size and format that is easiest to use and maintain is an important part of using the playbook to track and improve team performance.

Customizing the Playbook

Middle managers should customize their playbooks to suit their needs. The playbook is most useful when it captures the daily and weekly concerns of the middle manager. The nature and intent of a H.I.M.M. Playbook is to provide a quick reference for middle managers and their team members that, when used, helps the manager and team stay aligned and on track. Throughout the day, you should carry the playbook and update sections as needed. Examples of sections that you may want to add to the playbook include:

- Meetings to schedule or prepare
- Team-meeting discussion topics
- Phone numbers for important contacts
- Questions for peers or managers
- Areas needing research or analysis
- Action items that you have requested from others

By customizing your playbook, you will optimize the effectiveness and relevance of this tool and management practice. Each middle manager can tailor the playbook to meet his or her needs and complement his or her preferred planning style.

Creating a Departmental Strategic Plan: A Tutorial

Depending on your company's size and culture, you may or may not receive the training and coaching needed to create a departmental strategic plan. A departmental plan includes a departmental vision aligned with the corporate vision; three to five objectives that support corporate objectives; and goals, projects, and initiatives that produce those objectives. Each company may use different terminology, but don't worry about that. The exact names are not important. The importance of a plan is that it tells the middle manager and his or her team:

- Why they exist and the contribution they are expected to make to the corporation
- Their priorities and most important initiatives
- The plan for delivering the promised results

To get to this point, you, as a middle manager, need to learn and understand the corporate strategic plan and answer several questions about long-term and short-term needs, changes, and opportunities.

The following questions can be used to help brainstorm needs and considerations for a departmental strategic plan.

Long term: One to three years

- Based on the strategic plan (developed by senior management), what will be the purpose of this function over the next several years?
- How will the work change?
- What skills and resources will my team members need? How will these skills be developed in time to meet tomorrow's challenges?
- What changes should occur today to meet strategic goals?
- What are the major milestones over the next three years?
- What's coming down the pike and will it need attention?
- Will a different kind of management be required to produce different results? How should new skills be acquired and put into place?
- What is my department doing today that does not support the strategic direction?
- What should my team be working on to be aligned for future goals and initiatives?
- What do my team members need to know about the future direction?

Midterm: This year

- What does the company expect my team to accomplish this year? What are the team's deliverables? What are my team's current strengths and weaknesses?
- What will it take to deliver? What resources are required in the areas of people, roles, systems, processes, and projects?

- What should be included in the business plan and budget to achieve objectives?
- What changes will occur during the next year? Does my team have a clear change-implementation plan defined and in place?
- Does my team need to realign roles or processes to fulfill this year's business plan? Will my staff need new skills?
- What are the most important monthly and quarterly milestones? What business processes are required to ensure my department is aware of and focused on making these milestones?
- Are there decisions needed to enable the team to achieve its goals?

Short term: This month

- What is the work plan for the month? What key results does my team need to deliver? Can they get all of the work done? How will I communicate work plan progress?
- What are the barriers to my team's success? What is the plan for ensuring that barriers are defined and removed?
- Which metrics provide the best information about the team's productivity and results?
- What meetings should I schedule, plan, and lead to facilitate good communication, creativity, coordination, and/or problem solving?
- How should I spend my time to make the greatest impact?
- What coaching and/or development should I seek?
- How will I ensure that others make timely decisions affecting the team?
- What is my plan for coaching and developing my staff?

- What worries my team members, managers, and peers most? Who should I talk to about these concerns? Is there anything I have been putting off?

Weekly/daily

- What does my team need to accomplish today or this week and what's the plan for ensuring it all gets done?
- What are the problems and barriers getting in the way of productivity? Who should be working on these barriers? How can I remove barriers today?
- Who needs to be communicated with today?
- How should I spend my time today?
- Have I prepared today's meetings?

These questions, while a bit overwhelming, will help you brainstorm the type of information needed for the departmental strategic plan. Middle managers should be able to answer each question. This rough data will help you create the vision, objectives, and goals for your departmental plan. While formats and terms differ from company to company, here are definitions for each part of the departmental strategic plan:

The vision—The vision is a short statement, one to three sentences long, that states the main purpose for your team and the contribution it makes to the corporation. *Example:* The marketing department serves as the voice of the company in the marketplace. Marketing creates and conveys the company's brands, products, and services in ways that maximize market share, revenues, and customer satisfaction. The work of the marketing department is fundamental to the company's revenue generation and goals for market growth.

Objectives—Most departments should have three to five broad targets covering each major area or function within the department. Each objective should define the target, the completion timeline, and success measures. *Example:* Utilize the Web to improve product knowledge and market reach and to facilitate revenue generation. In the next year, implement two or three Web-based tools or products that generate revenue at an ROI of at least 10:1 (generate $10 in revenue for every $1 spent).

Goals—Most departmental plans contain two to five goals for each objective. Goals may be initiatives or projects. Goals must be specific, measurable, and have deadlines. *Example:* Develop and implement a plan for training distributors and wholesalers using Web-based technology. Complete forty training sessions with an average attendance of fifteen persons and an average ROI of 10:1 or better by the end of the year.

After creating a rough plan, you should review the plan in total to ensure that it is realistic. Departmental plans should be challenging and represent the work that can be accomplished when the team is highly productive. It is common to see departmental plans that are not practical or possible. Middle managers who create plans that contain too many projects or initiatives are setting their teams up for failure and frustration. If the objectives or projects are being requested by senior management, it may be necessary to negotiate the plan. Often it is a question of people and resources; many middle managers do not even bother to stand up for their teams when they are being asked to do more than is possible. Middle managers should do any or all of the following to ensure their plan is robust *and* doable:

- Challenge the conventional thinking. Is the plan really impossible? What if the department was reorganized or realigned?

- Negotiate the work. Are there projects or tasks that could be discontinued to allow new and higher-priority work to be completed? Be clear about what the department can and cannot do.
- Ask for more resources. Are new projects or initiatives important enough that they warrant additional and dedicated resources?
- Ask the team. Team members may offer great ideas for how the work can get done. They often know of ways to save resources and reduce waste.
- Ask peers for their ideas and input. Do they think the plan is unrealistic? What would they do if this were their plan?

Once the middle manager and senior management negotiate and agree to the plan, he or she should communicate it to all team members. The H.I.M.M. Playbook picks up where the departmental plan leaves off and is a daily tool that enables middle managers to stay on track with their plans.

Part Three

H.I.M.M. for Day-to-Day Execution

Chapter 6

Mucky Muck Obstructions—Navigating the Corporate Obstacle Course

MIDDLE MANAGERS LINK teams, systems, and processes together to produce results. This requires working with many different people and varied circumstances, which, in turn, can produce conflict, contradiction, and chaos—AKA mucky muck. Mucky muck causes a great deal of teeth-gnashing frustration, which is often reflected in comments such as:

- "Why is it so hard to get anything done around here?"
- "Why did I waste my time?"
- "Why wasn't I told that up-front?"
- "It takes forever to get a decision made in this company."
- "She and I just don't see eye to eye. I'll sit this one out."

Dealing with some mucky muck is an inevitable part of any job; however, unresolved mucky muck can quickly turn to quicksand that mires productivity, morale, and communication. To be successful as a middle manager, you need to be part investigator, part mind-reader, and part magician. Knowing how to navigate through corporate mucky muck is an essential middle-management skill.

The Sixteen Variations of Mucky Muck

The first step in getting through the mucky muck is to recognize what it looks like. Like various strains of virus, all mucky muck shares some common elements. Mucky muck is generally rooted in people's emotional and defensive reactions to feelings of personal censure or self-doubt. Other forms of mucky muck share an element of process, structure, or role getting in the way of common sense. Every work environment will breed and support different kinds of mucky muck; the following forms are the most common in many companies:

Variation #1: Miscommunication

Lou wondered why it was taking Mike so long to respond to his request for a few cost projections. He didn't know that Mike was upset because he thought that Lou was trying to usurp a portion of his territory. This was, in fact, not the case, but Mike responded emotionally to the perceived threat and thus had no incentive to help Lou.

Middle managers spend a surprisingly large amount of time clearing up confusion or hurt feelings that arise from miscommunication. E-mails are one of the biggest miscommunication generators because it is harder for the recipient to interpret the intent and tenor of brief written messages. To reduce the likelihood of miscommunication, make requests clear and specific, and provide examples to illustrate your meaning. Regularly talk in person or on the phone and resist the urge to assume that you know what others are thinking. To avoid this type of mucky muck, it is best to err on the side of overcommunicating with peers and team members.

Variation #2: Politics

Jim and his managers met with Jake to share their plan for the coming year. They knew they needed to get Jake's support before they presented their plan to the CEO. If the CEO knew that Jake supported the plan, he was less likely to reject it. It often worked best to have Jake share the plan with the CEO one-on-one to address his concerns before meeting with the management team. Although it took a few extra steps, this was the way Jim was best able to implement important changes.

The posturing and maneuvering that occur within a group or company are its politics. Nonpolitical managers, like Jim, are often forced to play politics to get things done. Gaining, keeping, or controlling power is often the motivation for politics. Managers who are political often think in hierarchical terms and show a preference for exclusivity. While politics are an inevitable part of many business environments, middle managers can reduce the negative impact of politics by learning the unwritten rules about how decisions are made. It is also important to ensure that you do not let concerns of status, ego, or self-preservation get in the way of your productivity. It is best to focus on the actions that will benefit work relationships and results.

Variation #3: Passing the buck and pointing fingers

Harry's boss asked him why one of his teams was short several staff members and was unable to meet its productivity goals. Harry had a problem supervisor who was causing people to walk off the job, but instead of being open about this, he blamed the problem on the HR department. Harry knew the root cause of this problem was that particular manager, and that he had neglected to do anything about it, hoping the situation would improve without his intervention.

Every day, middle managers face tough questions about their teams, processes, and results. If they suffer from low self-esteem and confidence, they, more often than not, will try to make sure they do not appear wrong or at fault in front of others. This may manifest itself in blaming their peers, managers, or, worse yet, subordinates for problems that have occurred. As one can imagine, this form of mucky muck breeds more obstacles, such as miscommunication and burned bridges. Middle managers who encounter this type of mucky muck should take the initiative to facilitate discussions where the facts and various perspectives can be heard. It is best to do this while maintaining a neutral and professional demeanor and by focusing on solving the problem (not on how you got into this situation).

Variation #4: Undiscussables

Several members of the senior management team drove back to the office after an all-day offsite strategic planning meeting. As was typical, the meeting had been fine but lacked any real value. The CEO and president asked for input but received only a watered-down version of the manager's ideas, concerns, and complaints. Three fears kept the managers from being honest about what they thought were the major problems in the company. First, they did not want to upset the CEO or president and make the rest of the day (and week) more difficult. Second, the managers did not feel comfortable saying they disagreed with some decisions that had been made by their bosses. Third, they feared that discussing their personal frustrations could damage their careers and standing with the executives.

Undiscussable topics may include feelings and opinions about the company, the work, or individual employees and customers. "Undiscussables" are common knowledge—such as the incompetent boss who got his promotion through nepotism, or the low salary scale that erodes morale and makes it impossible to retain the best employees—but they are not verbalized or publicly acknowledged. Undiscussables are those issues that people are thinking about but that are too delicate, embarrassing, uncomfortable, or scary to discuss openly in a group setting. The problem is that those issues *are* being discussed by staff at the watercooler, over lunch, and behind closed doors.

There are two ways in which middle managers can ensure that undiscussables don't get in the way of how they manage and lead. The first and more direct approach is to acknowledge the undiscussable. As a middle manager, you have the responsibility to be open and objective. This includes having the courage and conviction to take on tough topics. It is unlikely that you will lose your job or have your stature lowered for being open and honest (as long as your approach is constructive). Most undiscussables should be handled using the direct approach.

The second and less direct approach is to facilitate having certain individuals bring up the topic in the most palatable way. For example, a president once asked a particular board member to attend a planning meeting because he was certain the CEO would be more responsive to ideas offered by that board member. Granted, this approach smacks a little of politics, but in some work environments, it might be the most effective way for you to get results.

Variation #5: Disorganization

When Sally joined the company, it took her two months to sort through her predecessor's piles of paper and disorganized files to discover what was going on. Meanwhile, she missed several deadlines she was unaware even existed. There was no work plan or project calendar to reference. Middle managers who take over a new function often face this form of mucky muck. When misplaced data, buried files, or rarely seen desktops get in the way of completing a task, the work environment suffers from disorganization. Disorganization can affect an individual, a team, or an entire function or company. Middle managers can get a handle on disorganization by creating a team event around getting organized. Have a Friday-afternoon desk-cleanout event or a once-a-month organizing extravaganza. What you don't want to do is let getting organized wait—there may be something important and urgent on the bottom of one of those stacks of paper.

Variation #6: Learned helplessness

Tim was struck by how listless, compliant, and dependent several of his employees were. They seemed like intelligent and dedicated people but did not demonstrate an ability to think independently or to be enthusiastic about the work. Tim learned the previous two managers discouraged initiative and rewarded those who were compliant. Many in Tim's group demonstrated learned helplessness, which occurs when a person or group accepts a certain reality based on previous experiences or information. In the corporate environment, learned helplessness is common, and is most often faced by middle managers who take over managing a new team of people who had previously not performed well. Learned helplessness can be unlearned when the middle manager communicates and clarifies expectations and roles, and then follows up with training and reinforcement of the new expectations. By frequently asking employees for their input and creativity (versus being directive), middle managers can help raise the expectations the employees have of themselves.

Variation #7: Hidden agendas

Debbie called a meeting with the marketing and product managers to share her idea for a new product. Though her concept was interesting, the managers could not help but wonder about her real motivation for the proposed change. Perhaps what she really wanted was for her group to produce the new product because she thought it would be more exciting and interesting than the product they were supposed to launch next year.

Middle managers often work with people who have hidden agendas. Hidden agendas become a problem when they get in the way of others' doing their jobs or relating in a genuine way. The reason a person acts a certain way or makes a particular decision is often a mystery. However, hidden agendas often revolve around power, being right, getting ahead, looking good with the boss, covering up a failure, or gaining support for a pet project. Hidden agendas can often be revealed by asking open-ended questions about the intent, benefits, and evolution of the idea or project. A middle manager's objective is not necessarily to eliminate hidden agendas, but rather to understand them so that he or she can make a well-informed decision.

Variation #8: Long-term alliances

Corky had done her homework. Her detailed and well-researched proposal recommended changing a major employee-benefit vendor. Making the change would save the company money and would provide better service to the employees. It seemed to be a win-win situation. Little did Corky know that the current vendor, which charged premium rates and provided only average service, had a long-standing personal relationship with the president. Sure enough, what should have been a foolproof proposal failed miserably. Because middle managers interact with managers at all levels of the organization, it is inevitable that they will encounter this breed of mucky muck. Old relationships or alliances can thwart productivity when they get in the way of sound business decisions or make the workplace dysfunctional.

The best defense against being blindsided by long-term alliances is to ask questions early in the project-planning process.

Variation #9: Burned bridges

Lou was mortified. He had accidentally sent an e-mail disparaging a coworker to that very coworker! Though Lou apologized, he could not reverse the damage done to the relationship. As a middle manager, you may need to deal with burned bridges—be it your own or those of others in your department. Burned bridges get in the way of future communication and collaboration. The problem can get worse when other employees in the department get embroiled in the messy matter. To prevent burning a bridge with a peer or manager, never say or write anything that you would not feel comfortable repeating to that person directly. In particular, resist the urge to send inflammatory or emotional e-mails.

Variation #10: Clashes in style

Dana and Sally were intelligent and dedicated managers who could not communicate effectively with each other. They conversed with each other in patronizing and disrespectful tones. However, when they worked with other people, everything was fine. The breakdown occurred only when they interacted with each other. Why did Dana and Sally have this problem? Their communication and behavioral styles clashed so severely that they annoyed each other and were unable to communicate effectively. They also lacked mutual respect for each other, which often accompanies a clash in styles.

High impact middle managers need to be part psychologist and part mediator when faced with employees or coworkers whose styles clash and get in the way of their working relationship. Unfortunately, this makes work more difficult for everyone who has to compensate for those individuals. If you focus on the task at hand and not on the way in which the other person presents himself or herself, you will be more successful in dealing with clashes in style. Recognizing and being open about style differences will help disarm the power and magnitude of the clash.

Variation #11: Disempowerment

Overwhelmed and in danger of losing her job, Jane was not getting her work done on time. Jane's employees, on the other hand, had time and capacity to spare. In particular, Kathy had a strong background and work experience that could have helped Jane with several of the larger projects she was unable to complete on schedule. In fact, based on the scope of Kathy's job, at least one of the projects should have been her responsibility in the first place, but Jane chose to take it on herself because the work was inter- esting. Had Jane asked her to, Kathy could have done much of the work and planning, and the project would have been completed on time. Middle managers who disempower their employees lessen their intrinsic motivation and job satisfaction. It also causes role ambiguity, workflow disruptions, and miscommunication.

Disempowerment also results in workload problems for the manager who is taking on more than he or she should. To recognize and reduce the effects of disempowerment, middle managers should periodically review roles and team-member workloads with their manager and team. For each to-do item on your list, ask the question, "Should I be doing this or does it belong on someone else's list?"

Variation #12: Contradictory information

Mike was frustrated because he was not getting answers about why sales of third-party products had dropped dramatically from last year. Lou and Tim, the middle managers in charge of this revenue stream, were supposed to provide analysis and an action plan for getting back on track. The problem was that Tim and Lou did not see the significant drop that Mike did. In fact, some of their data suggested that sales had actually improved from the previous year. The accounting department was working on providing a new and more accurate report, but they were running into contradictions and inconsistencies in the data. Two months had passed and Mike worried that the opportunity to fix the situation would evaporate; meanwhile, Lou and Tim weren't even convinced that a problem existed. Middle managers spend countless hours trying to find and validate the information they use to make decisions. Working with contradictory information is frustrating and wastes precious time. Worse yet, incorrect information can cause major errors in judgment and decisions. Middle managers who ask questions about how information is collected and take the initiative to analyze important measurements within their function are less likely to be impacted by contradictory information. It is rarely a good strategy to assume that no news is good news concerning fundamental business processes.

Variation #13: Duplication of efforts

Todd talked to Jake about creating an auditing process to ensure that products were meeting customer expectations. Lilly, as part of her overall product planning and improvement responsibilities, was also working on a new auditing process. When Lilly found out that Todd had gone to Jake with his idea for the auditing process, she asked Todd why he was working on it. Todd said that he saw a need and took it upon himself to put together a plan. He did not know that Lilly planned to create and implement a similar process. Together, they eventually worked it out so only one process was developed, but in the interim everyone's valuable time was wasted. It was also uncomfortable for Lilly, who felt as though Todd had taken initiative outside his area of responsibility.

Middle managers' responsibilities often overlap, but duplications of effort are wasteful and disruptive to the organization. Sometimes, as in the example of Lilly and Todd, duplication occurs because of misinformation. Other times, duplications occur because one manager does not have confidence in another—a hidden agenda for sure! Peers who regularly get together to share projects and priorities are less likely to get tripped up by duplications of effort. In addition, middle managers should know and respect each other's roles and areas of responsibility.

Variation #14: Sticks-in-the-mud

Charlie had been with the company a long time and remembered when it had been much smaller and easier to manage. Anytime a new idea for automating information or processes came up, Charlie would balk. He didn't believe that the company needed to go to such lengths. He believed the methods of yesterday would serve the current organization just as well. Not all sticks-in-the-mud are long-term employees reminiscing about the "old days"; however, they *do* share a dislike of change and a leeriness toward new approaches. Middle managers who face this type of mucky muck spend more time and energy enrolling others in change efforts.

Sticks-in-the-mud can get in the way of progress and make implementing new ideas more difficult. Middle managers can deal with change-resistant people by frequently communicating the purpose, plan, and staff roles relative to the change. You need to make sure that all employees understand the change and the reasons for it. Much resistance is born out of misinformation. Ultimately, change-resistant employees should not be allowed to sabotage or get in the way of changes that have been agreed to.

Variation #15: Group defections

Ron and his management team made all the right comments when they participated in companywide training meetings. They even seemed positive and optimistic about announced changes. However, when they returned to their workplace, it was as if none of those conversations had taken place. Ron's management team decided they would do the work their own way and ignore any direction from the home office that they found unappealing. Together, they essentially defected from the overall management team and became their own entity. As a result, their division did not reflect the overall vision of the company and employees who transferred to their unit from other departments did not do well.

Group defections are more common in corporate America than one would think, and they cause breaks in communication, work inefficiencies, and lower morale and employee satisfaction. Middle managers can eliminate group defections by ensuring that they spend time with each of their work teams and handle concerns and problems proactively. It is not enough to manage through e-mails and staff meetings. High impact middle managers know what's going on in the groups they manage because they spend quality time building formal and informal relationships and partnerships with each team and manager.

Variation #16: Sabotage

Deirdre knew it was not going to work. She had told the management team before they implemented the new process that her group was less efficient and felt confused by the new procedures. Other groups had implemented the new automated process with few problems and had reduced processing times using the new system. Deirdre's manager, Bob, felt that she had caused the project to fail by disparaging the change to her team. Deirdre practiced a form of subtle sabotage when she spoke negatively about the change to her employees. She even encouraged them to help her amass evidence to keep things the way they were. Most middle managers have experienced sabotage at one time or another. The most common forms of sabotage are negative and inappropriate comments about changes or decisions that have been made. Sabotage harms productivity, communication, and morale. Middle managers can reduce the likelihood of sabotage by being highly visible and accessible during times of change and by monitoring change implementation closely. Visibility will increase the manager's opportunity to observe the subtle clues that indicate a team member is not doing his or her part to support the change.

Do any of these forms of mucky muck look familiar? There is a practical reason for classifying these barriers as mucky muck. Each represents weak, immature, or shortsighted behavior on the part of an individual, group, or company. Mucky muck does not make sense—it just is. This is not to say that it does not matter or cause damage. In some work environments, the mucky muck is so thick that it drives smart people away or causes them to fail. Characterizing these examples of corporate folly will help you tackle it. In addition, when called "mucky muck," a ridiculous name to be sure, its power dwindles. Like calling a seven-foot bodybuilder "Tiny," calling these barriers "mucky muck" lessens their ability to intimidate. Mucky muck is inevitable, but you can have a significant impact on how much mucky muck there is and how your staff responds to it.

Eleven Techniques for Navigating Mucky Muck

Teams rely on their managers to cut through the mucky muck and help them get their jobs done. Middle managers are most likely to face mucky muck because they interact with more functions, levels, groups, and individuals than others in the company do. Once mucky muck presents itself, you can reduce its power over your department and organization. High impact middle managers have figured out how to respond to mucky muck so it does not get in the way of results. H.I.M.M. techniques for navigating include the following:

Technique #1: Do the right homework.

Jim and his team needed to come up with a strategic business plan for the coming year. They knew that senior management had several preconceived ideas about what the plan should look like. Rather than wasting their time creating a plan that only represented what they thought the priorities should be, they first sought to understand the senior managers' points of view and then developed their plan. Some might say this approach was faulty because Jim and his team circumscribed their own ideas to those of senior management. While this may be true, the team knew that senior management had already made up their minds about what they thought needed to happen. They knew that they could most help the organization by developing a plan that implemented senior management's ideas in the best possible way. In the end, they were able to influence several aspects of the plan much more so than they would have had they not been sensitive to the agendas that senior management wanted.

As a middle manager, you will face situations like this on a regular basis. If there are strong opinions or relationships influencing a decision-maker, it is best to do your homework and discover what they are before wasting too much time working in the opposite direction. Before starting a project, ask yourself, "Is there historical information that would be helpful to know? What are senior management's thoughts on this project? What approaches have been suggested in the past? Are there preferred vendors or partners that should be maintained?" There may be times when this added work and research is not necessary and unencumbered creative thinking is possible. However, it is always better to err on the side of being prepared.

Technique #2: Pick and choose your battles.

Ann knew that she was right about the benefits of changing to a different vendor and that she had presented a thorough case to her bosses. Ann felt the decision to turn down her proposal was not logical. She did not want to let go of her idea, but in the end, she realized it was not a battle worth fighting. The current vendor cost more and did not provide the high level of service the proposed vendor would, but overall the service they received was satisfactory. Nothing terrible was going to happen by keeping the current vendor. There would be bigger and more important battles to fight another day, and Ann knew it was better to let this one go.

Middle managers often face the decision whether to hold firm and fight for what they think is right or accept another decision and move on. If you wage too many battles, you may end up commanding less respect in your organization. In addition, your message will seem watered down and ineffective. Like the story of the boy who cried wolf, if you tout every proposal or idea as critically important, you will eventually find that the truly important projects will be ignored or be seen as being unworthy of special consideration. High impact middle managers know how to choose their battles and use their influence for maximum gain and importance.

Technique #3: Focus energy where it will count.

Tracy and her team knew there were a few departments that were not receptive to the coaching and development she and her team could provide. She offered their services to all departments but focused on working with the few groups that showed interest in, and would benefit most from, their support. At any time, the other groups could change their mind and receive help as well. Tracy recognized that the saying "You can lead a horse to water, but you can't make it drink" also applied to individual managers and teams. By not forcing her support on the managers who were obviously not interested in working with her, Tracy was able to spend her time in a way that was more fruitful and satisfying.

Middle managers work hard to have a positive influence on as broad an audience as possible. When individuals or groups show that they are not receptive, focus your efforts in another direction. This, of course, is not always possible. If a middle manager finds his or her direct reports are not receptive to his or her management, he or she needs to address and fix the problem. If, on the other hand, there are several possible projects to propose and work on, it is wise to consider which will receive more collaboration and cooperation when deciding how to manage your and your team's time and resources.

Technique #4: Overcommunicate, be inclusive, and follow up.

Lou assumed that other managers understood his role and the functions he had ownership of. It is rarely safe to assume this kind of interdepartmental understanding exists. A better approach for Lou would have been to communicate more frequently and to a wider audience about the projects and initiatives he and his group were undertaking. All middle managers should err on the side of overcommunication to reduce the likelihood of miscommunication, duplication of work, and contradictory information.

Technique #5: Analyze and fix it.

When Mike joined the company as controller, it was fraught with contradictory financial information and inaccurate reports. He rolled up his sleeves, dug into the numerical mess, and fixed many of the problems with the data. Mike also oversaw the creation of several reports that helped managers run their parts of the business more effectively. When faced with contradictory information, duplication of efforts, or miscommunication, great middle managers do whatever it takes to understand and solve the problem. Good analysis goes a long way toward reducing or eliminating these and other types of mucky muck.

Technique #6: Ask probing questions to reveal motives and hidden agendas.

Mindy was an intuitive manager who knew the right questions to ask in order to discover people's real intent and motivation. At one meeting, a manager was recommending that they restructure several roles. Mindy asked several questions to determine this manager's motive for recommending the change. Privately, she speculated whether his agenda was to increase the size of his organization, or if he thought the current department manager was doing a poor job. Mindy's open-ended questions helped to clarify the details of his recommendation. High impact middle managers know when and how to ask the right questions that help explain the intent and motivation behind others' comments and ideas.

Technique #7: Repair relationships.

John and Barry knew that their relationship was dysfunctional, but it was not until they were honest with each other that they were able to repair the relationship and work together more effectively. Once they resolved the issues between them, both of their departments experienced less mucky muck.

It can be uncomfortable and difficult, but it is important for you to repair damaged relationships with current employees or coworkers. When not dealt with, these poor relationships will get in the way of communication, workflow, and results. Repairing a relationship does not mean that you have to socialize with each other; it means being able to work together productively and collaboratively. Workplace relationships should facilitate rather than hinder productive work.

Technique #8: Believe in the capacity people have for change and learning.

If Tim had not looked past his employees' learned helplessness, he might have written them off as poor performers. Instead, he created a work environment that nurtured creativity and initiative. It took a while, but most of the previously lethargic employees became more engaged and passionate about their work. They accepted the changes that Tim was implementing and offered ideas for additional improvements. Great middle managers know that most performance problems are actually management or system problems and that given the right guidance and leadership, nearly all employees will have the desire and capacity to do a great job. Mucky muck can get in the way of people's working at their best, but the damage does not have to be permanent.

Technique #9: Get organized.

When Sally started her new job, she took over for a deeply disorganized manager. The first couple of months were difficult for Sally and she felt set up to fail. Mucky muck that comes from disorganization is common but is also the easiest to fix. Once Sally created a filing system and routine that worked for her, she gained control of her department and became productive and successful. High impact middle managers know that they need to stay organized to ensure that they and their teams are efficient and feel confident about their work. Whether done daily, weekly, or as needed, creating and practicing methods for organizing work is an important middle-manager skill (Chapters 7 and 8 offer several techniques for staying organized).

Technique #10: Lighten up and roll with it.

Tim was an intense middle manager who let mucky muck frustrate him. He asked why things had to be a certain way or why it wasn't easier to get work done. This emotional reaction got in the way of his moving past the mucky muck and getting his job done. It would have been better for him to shrug his shoulders, chuckle a bit, and rethink how to get the work done. Like Tim, some middle managers take mucky muck too seriously. They get upset about the inefficiencies and frustration it causes, which keeps them from being able to navigate through it. When dealing with mucky muck, the first action you can take is to see it for the ridiculous barrier that it is. The middle managers who prevail despite it all are able to quickly move beyond the barriers. They know there are many ways to make a difference and that they can do great work even when faced with mucky muck. Sometimes, the best approach is just to laugh at it and move on.

Technique #11: See and enjoy accomplishments.

Jim was lamenting to Lou about how hard it was to work in their organization because of all the mucky muck he faced daily. Lou agreed but chose to see it another way. Although Jim was right about the mucky muck, Lou saw the situation as inspiring and hopeful. They had a great middle-management team that accomplished much under difficult working conditions. They had been successful in creating major change and improvements within a work environment that was rife with politics, disorganization, and other permutations of mucky muck. What an accomplishment! Moreover, they were learning skills that would benefit their careers and enable them to prevail in almost any work environment. Yes, it was frustrating, and yes, getting things done should not have been so hard, but the success of the team was worthy of celebration. Middle managers who produce results and get through the mucky muck should recognize and take pride in the work they do and the results they achieve against the odds.

High impact middle managers practice these eleven techniques to reduce and eliminate mucky muck from their work environment. They try to bring perspective to each challenge and strengthen weak communication channels that are often at the core of mucky muck. These techniques are also excellent methods for managing other complex or emotionally charged situations. Once you practice seeing and managing mucky muck, you will become skilled at recognizing emerging problems and preventing them from undermining morale and derailing projects.

Be Part of the Solution, Not the Problem

As a high impact middle manager, you need to be careful that you do not become a mucky muck generator. Now that it is clear what mucky muck is and how it damages productivity and results, you have the responsibility of owning the mucky muck you create and eliminating it. There are significant benefits of doing so. First, your work will be more meaningful and successful when not deluged with self-inflicted mucky muck. Second, middle managers who ensure they do not become part of the problem will enjoy others' respect and trust. To make your workplace productive, practice the following strategies:

- Plan and communicate in clear and complete terms.
- Communicate openly and candidly with managers, peers, and employees.
- Understand the motivations and intentions behind ideas and suggestions. Share them honestly.
- Share projects and initiatives with peers at the formative stage of planning and implementation.
- Be a good corporate citizen. Represent the company and management well.
- Support employees so they can fully take on and own the work appropriate to their job.

Don't:
- Gossip or badmouth others.
- Obstruct or otherwise subtly sabotage changes.
- Allow differences in style or personality to get in the way of working productively with a peer or employee.
- Interfere or take over a project or task that one of your employees owns.
- Let work pile up or become disorganized.
- Play favorites or make business decisions based on friendship.

By following these guidelines, you can have an immediate and positive impact on your work environment. Mucky muck can be full of uncomfortable emotions and dealing with this is draining. Reducing mucky muck frees up mental and physical energy that can be used to do great work. Start calling these barriers mucky muck in the presence of others and notice how referring to it in this silly manner can help reduce its power and importance.

Chapter 7

H.I.M.M. Organizational Alignment— Ensuring the Department Delivers Results

A WELL-ALIGNED DEPARTMENT hums with efficiency. Processes for getting the work done are clearly understood and effective. Staff members' roles support the goals of both the team and the company. Individuals are clear about what they should contribute. They are appropriately empowered and held accountable for producing results. Communication to and from departments facilitates each team's ability to remain on course and prioritize. The organizational structure and individual roles enable team members to identify and solve problems quickly. Work is more satisfying because it makes sense.

On the other hand, poorly aligned organizational structures and processes cause numerous problems with quality, throughput, and results. When a structure or process is out of alignment with the larger goal it was designed to support, it no longer serves the goals of the team and company. Poor alignment can occur for various reasons. Perhaps changes have occurred in one area of the organization, but not in others. Sometimes the problem is a lack of effective processes for getting the work done. Or it could be that roles have changed but processes have not, or visa versa.

A common reason for poor alignment is conflict among technology, processes, and roles. For team members, a poorly aligned organization feels disorganized, and getting work done seems more difficult than it should. Ambiguous, confusing, and overlapping roles are also signs of poor alignment. The design and planning of workflow is significant and should be a major focus for middle managers. Many middle managers, however, assume that unproductive people are to blame for poor results. While there may be personnel problems for the manager to resolve, it is more likely that the department's processes and structures are responsible for poor results.

Elements of Organizational Structure

The organizational structure defines job roles, departmental interdependencies, and communication channels. Structure determines who makes the decisions, and the depth and breadth of each person's role. Structure assigns responsibilities and accountabilities. The H.I.M.M. definition of middle manager is someone who oversees and is responsible for at least one structure/function that exists within the larger company structure. A middle manager who leads the sales and marketing departments may oversee a sales organization structure, a marketing structure, and one or more cross-functional project teams with their own structure. The HR director may oversee one large structure that encompasses the entire department with several smaller structures supporting the functions of recruiting, benefits, and training.

Processes are ways of working within a structure. They may be as elaborate and complicated as a computer controlled manufacturing line or as simple as a way to deliver mail throughout an office. There are also de facto processes, or processes that have evolved and become standard practice without intentional design or planning. Most middle managers oversee several processes. Inefficient or irrelevant processes hurt results and cause productivity to suffer. This chapter will help middle managers ensure that they have the right structure and processes in place to produce results.

As a high impact middle manager you should continuously evaluate and realign structures and processes. Doing so will give you and your team the best chance for success. When results are inadequate, ask yourself, your team members, and your peers if the way the work is being done is enabling, or getting in the way of, results. Are the processes and procedures that have been established setting you up for success or failure?

Best Practices for Organizational Alignment

H.I.M.M. organizational alignment is a set of practices that enable middle managers to keep their structures and processes relevant and productive. These practices begin by looking at your department, and the work it produces, from a 50,000-foot-high view, or broad perspective, to answer one fundamental question: Is this department set up for success? High impact middle managers regularly look at their functions in this way because they know that keeping roles and processes aligned is critical to ensuring optimal throughput and results. Once the big picture is clear, you can begin to focus on aspects of the structures and processes that need attention to deliver results. H.I.M.M. organizational alignment should:

- Clarify the vision, purpose, and goals for the department
- Use clean-slate creativity to design an ideal organization model

- Compare the needs of the department, the ideal organization model, and current roles and processes
- Generate alternatives that improve the organization
- Realign structure, processes, roles, and procedures for maximum efficiency
- Measure and monitor processes and workflow

H.I.M.M. organizational alignment will help you ensure that your work structures and processes mesh in a way that enables team members to be their most productive and deliver results.

Practice #1: Clarify the vision, purpose, and goals for the department.

The middle manager, his or her manager, and his or her team should all agree on the vision for the department's success and the expectations the company has for the department (refer to Chapter 5). These expectations should represent the needs and wants of both internal and external customers. Here is an example of what the vision, purpose, and goals might look like for an accounting department:

The accounting department is an internal service group and has an opportunity and responsibility to provide responsive and helpful service to both internal and external customers. This includes providing accurate and timely information, proactive analysis, resolutions of problems, and response to questions. There is also an expectation that, as the accounting experts, the department staff will ensure the company is following proper procedures to ensure fiscal accuracy and compliance with important regulations and audit principles. As the company expands its presence on the Internet, it is expecting the accounting function to support and reconcile business transactions produced via the Web. Over the next year, the accounting team's major goals are to:

- Improve the efficiency of invoice processing in order to reduce errors by 50 percent and improve processing speed by 15 percent while maintaining or improving current processing costs.
- Improve purchasing and payment processes related to field operations so that communications and information exchange are more efficient and the cost of the processing is reduced by 10 percent or more.
- Design and launch accurate and helpful reports that enable department managers to manage their areas more proactively and effectively. This effort should lead to an overall reduction in budget variances by the third month of implementation.
- Create and implement, by June, a strategy that supports the company's plans for selling products and services on its Web site. Develop online cash register services and reconciliation methods to ensure the proper collection and management of revenues.

The statement of the vision, purpose, and goals for a department is an important tool for middle managers. It should become part of the department's playbook (see Chapter 5) and be posted for employees, peers, and managers to see. When you take the time, as a middle manager, to crystallize and clarify your department's vision, purpose, and goals, you build a foundation for creating organizational alignment.

Practice #2: Use clean-slate creativity to design an ideal organization model.

To realign structures and processes, it is important to start the design process with a clean slate before considering current resources, processes, and roles. Using clean-slate creativity means designing, from the ground up, the ideal way a team and processes should function to produce the vision and goals (see sidebar for more details). For this exercise, do not think about current personnel, roles, resources, or processes. Instead, you should define how the work would be designed if nothing were already in place. Hence the clean-slate metaphor. The following questions will help get your creative juices flowing:

- What is the long-term direction of the company, and how should the manager and team design today's work with this in mind?
- What is the most important work this team could do?
- What needs to be accomplished to meet or exceed the team's goals? Look at each goal individually, then as a whole.
- To do this work, what roles are required? How should the department divide work among individuals and teams?
- How should managers and team members make decisions?
- What should the key processes be and how should they work? What processes would make the work easier and more efficient?
- What role should technology play?
- How would the team and process link to the rest of the company?
- What are the advantages and disadvantages of this organizational design?
- What human, process, and technology resources are needed to make this organization structure work?
- If there were no limitations on resources, how would you and your team design the department's structure?

If it is feasible, you may find it helpful to have the entire team contribute to creating this design. The product of this creative work is an ideal view of what the organization and work processes would look like if designed from scratch to produce the vision, purpose, and goals of the department. In addition to clarifying the roles, it is important to identify the processes that would make the work of the team easier and more efficient. Depending on the scope and breadth of the work you are assessing, this exercise could take several hours or even days.

Clean-Slate Creativity Versus Problem Solving

»» There are two distinct ways you, as a middle manager, can approach a situation that needs improvement. You can choose clean-slate creativity or employ a problem-solving approach. In using the clean-slate approach, define how you would manage the work if there were no processes currently in place and no limitations on resources. To be successful using this method, do not let your ideas become bogged down or hampered by current processes, people, or corporate culture. You can recognize current resources and limitations later in the redesign process.

When using a problem-solving approach, begin with today's roles, processes, and circumstances, and then define ways to improve results or performance from this current reality. Ideas conceived using this approach will more likely be similar and complementary to the work and processes your department is already using. Thus, the problem-solving approach works best when your department needs to make only minor changes or adjustments, not redesign an organization or process. Ideas that come from clean-slate creativity will be more innovative, more creative, and more likely to lead to significant improvements in productivity.

Middle managers should complete this exercise for their entire department at least once every two years, and then follow up with smaller redesign efforts for specific areas as needed. For example, if your company launches a new product line, a portion of the department's work and processes may need realignment. If there is one available, having a facilitator guide you and your team through these conversations is often helpful and allows a middle manager to participate fully.

Practice #3: Compare department needs, the ideal plan, and current roles and processes.

Once the ideal organizational design is complete, middle managers will be ready to bring the current reality into the realignment process and conversation. It is important to include a discussion of de facto processes, meaning processes you and your team have not purposefully designed or implemented but that have developed over time. There are generally many more processes in place than middle managers recognize. For example, communication and problem resolution are areas where de facto processes are common.

During this part of the realignment, you will need to blend the ideal scenario with current roles, personnel, and processes. There is always going to be some give-and-take and some compromise required. It is important to stand firm and resolute for the changes that are most important and be flexible and nimble in areas where multiple approaches might work. You and your team should ask and answer the following questions:

- How far apart are the ideal organization model and the current organization? What are the differences and similarities?
- Is the ideal organization possible and practical?
- If the ideal organization is worth attaining, what might a transitional organization look like? How can the department begin its journey to ideal alignment?
- What aspects of the current organization and processes should not be changed? Challenge the thinking behind the

answers to these questions. Why should these processes or roles stay the same?

- What further information or research do you and your team need to understand these ideas and choices? (Do this analysis and research before making decisions.)
- What objections or concerns will senior management or peers have about these ideas? Are they valid? How can you and your team overcome these objections?

Again, using a facilitator to guide you and your team through this process is helpful and advised. A facilitator can see where the team is getting bogged down or where its thinking might need to be challenged. If a facilitator is not available, you will need to do a thorough job of planning the agenda and discussion questions before the meeting. After this conversation, you will know the ideas on the table and the pros and cons of each. You will also have a good idea of how much needs to change to create alignment. This is a useful and illuminating process.

A word about team-member participation: The general rule is that you should include input from team members and peers as much as possible. Depending on the nature of the realignment, it may not be appropriate to include team members in discussions about redesigning roles and processes. If jobs might be eliminated, then team members should not participate in the final design of roles. If team members ask whether jobs might be cut (they are probably wondering even if they do not ask), it is best to be open and honest. You can say that the purpose of the organizational realignment and redesign is to figure out how the department can be more efficient and effective. This may mean that some processes and jobs will change or be affected, but the final details will not be clear until the realignment plan is complete and approved. If people are likely to be impacted, middle managers should get through the redesign process as quickly as possible. If the organizational realignment is going to be significant and include major role changes, it might be best to complete the entire redesign process confidentially and without team-member participation. Middle managers who do not include team members in the redesign process should take extra care and caution to ensure they are getting thorough and accurate information with which to make decisions.

Practice #4: Generate alternatives for organizational improvement.

As a middle manager, you should create two or three realignment approaches based on the information collected and discussion that has occurred. If there is one alternative that seems significantly better than the other possible plans, then present only one plan. Because more than one workable scenario often exists, it is generally best to prepare and present more than one option. As the planning progresses, you may eliminate choices based on several criteria, including cost, ease of use, technology, or mucky muck. The exception to this rule is when the middle manager and team feel confident and positive about an organizational design they have created. If you have done your homework and included the appropriate people in discussions, then present this recommendation and sell it to the key stakeholders and decision-makers. Energy and passion account for much of the success of any plan. Whether presenting one or more alternatives, each plan should include:

- A review of the vision, purpose, and goals the realignment seeks to support
- The major reasons the realignment is necessary
- A review of the proposed realigned organization and processes, and the results that the proposed organization will produce

- Transition plans for personnel roles and processes that would change
- A description of roles and interdependencies between team members
- A description of major processes
- An explanation of how the work will flow from and to other groups
- A breakdown of costs, including short-term and long-term cost effects

Depending on the scope of the plan, preparing it could take anywhere from a few hours to a couple of weeks. For a narrow focus area or single process, the entire realignment can take less than a day. Don't rush the process if more analysis and creativity will make the plan significantly richer or better. As the plan is coming together, middle managers should play the devil's advocate and encourage team members to challenge it to ensure that it answers potential objections and meets the needs of supporters and potential naysayers. Present the options to several trusted peers and ask for their input. Adjust the plan as appropriate.

Present the plan and gain approval! Provide backup information and details as needed. Have this information ready and available when others ask questions. Take the time to prepare for the presentation of the plan, as this will speed up its approval. Be open to adjusting the plan to get full support.

Practice #5: Realign structure, processes, roles, and procedures.

The implementation of new structures and processes is critical to the success of the realignment. To ensure that team members and peers support the new way of doing the work, middle managers should:

- Work with management and HR on the timing of the plan's implementation, especially if any individual jobs or positions are affected.

- Communicate the vision, the realignment plan, the transition plan, and the role of each team member. Discuss the plan with peers and gain their support. If an individual's job is changing significantly, talk to him or her one-on-one before any team announcements.

- Create a project plan for the transition of roles and processes. Ensure that all team members and affected peers have a current copy of the plan. Hold daily or weekly progress chats as needed.

- Be sincerely open and ready to listen to any concerns, suggestions, or questions. Be flexible enough to accept that the plan may need to be altered. Take time every day to check in with team members and peers. Do not micromanage the process, but show support and invite feedback.

Practice #6: Measure and monitor processes and workflow.

As the realignment rolls out and takes hold, it is important to monitor and measure performance and productivity. After all, that is why changes were made in the first place! Measures should be communicated clearly and discussed often. As well as being part of the departmental playbook, key measures and milestones should be posted in a visible place in the department. If team members are located in the field, you can send, and discuss, measures and results to each team member as part of regular e-mail and telephone conversations.

Ensuring that your department is set up for success is important work for middle managers. Team members are more productive and satisfied when roles and processes facilitate results. In an aligned organization, mucky muck goes down and the work environment is more intrinsically motivating.

An aligned organization runs like a well-oiled machine. High impact middle managers know that, in order to ensure their teams are set up for success, processes and roles need to be evaluated regularly as changes occur. When processes are inefficient, they produce waste and cause team members to work harder to get results. When roles are unclear or do not encompass new expectations, team members cannot do their best work. The H.I.M.M. organizational alignment will help middle managers efficiently get results.

Chapter 8

H.I.M.M. Leaders Are Unstoppable! — Wiping Out Limitations to Results

TALENTED AND CREATIVE, Marty was a great catch for the company. He was hired to take over the leadership of an internal service department that was not meeting its deadlines and was producing low-quality work. Marty had the right vision and understood the importance of delivering high-quality work that was on time and on budget. Thus, Marty's managers were puzzled when the timeliness of the department's work went from bad to worse under Marty's management.

To ensure that the planning, timeliness, and quality of the work were acceptable, Marty oversaw and reviewed all the work his group produced. Everything flowed through Marty and relied on his stamp of approval. Because quality was an issue and Marty wanted to develop his team's ability to recognize and solve problems, he reworked many of the projects himself. The quality of the work improved, but the completion rate was getting worse because Marty micromanaged every project. Marty also needed to spend time evaluating vendors and creating a long-term strategic plan for the department. There was not enough Marty to go around, and his involvement in projects had become a constraint.

Paul, another manager in Marty's organization, felt stuck. He needed to create and implement a plan to upgrade his team's skills and professionalism, but he put off the work again and again. He turned down help when it was offered. Time slipped away and he did not have his plan ready or implemented in time for the next hiring season. Paul didn't know how to plan well. He had the tendency to be reactive instead of proactive, and he was often uncoachable when the topic of planning or time management came up. Paul often let the needs of the day divert his attention, and he never got around to completing the plan.

Corky knew she needed to get candidates through the selection and hiring process more quickly and efficiently, but she was at a loss about where to start. The selection and hiring process had many parts, each a potential place for breakdowns and delays. The application flow was good, but sometimes the applications sat for a while before anyone had time to review them. At times, interviews took longer than expected because of schedule conflicts. Reference checks, background checks, and drug screenings took more time than Corky preferred, but these processes relied on outside vendors who would not commit to faster results. The best candidates also needed to give their current employer two weeks' notice before leaving. Corky wondered what changes she could make that would optimize the hiring process while taking into account the resources available to her.

Maximizing Throughput

Marty, Paul, and Corky struggled with challenges that limited their results. Maximizing throughput to deliver products and services is an important responsibility of all middle managers. Throughput is the rate at which a person, department, system, or function produces results. Throughput may be expressed in terms of speed, quantity, time, or a combination of these factors. Most work can be described in terms of throughput. The time it takes to make decisions is throughput. The number of completed calls may be throughput. The accuracy of completed payroll check runs is throughput. Even manager capacity can be thought of in terms of throughput.

Middle managers are in the best position to recognize and resolve problems that limit throughput because they see and interact with many levels and layers of work, systems, and processes. In addition, it makes sense that middle managers be concerned with and interested in throughput since throughput leads to results. Middle managers are often the most directly accountable for producing results. Focusing on and improving throughput may come naturally for some middle managers; those who come from a traditional manufacturing or product distribution background are most likely to have had experience in this area. Many middle managers, however, have had neither training nor experience in solving throughput problems.

A disciplined and focused day-to-day management practice is essential to understanding and improving throughput. Factors that limit throughput may change daily or be a continuing problem. In either case, middle managers prepared to quickly identify and deal with these problems get better results. Middle managers must seek out and resolve barriers to throughput using analysis, conversation, observation, and interactive MBWA (Management By Walking Around).

What Reduces Throughput?

Several common business practices and actions can limit throughput. Sometimes, making one change can improve throughput; at other times, combining several actions will work best. You should also be cautious that making a change in one area does not cause problems in other areas. There are several ways to look at throughput and each offers a unique view of potential problems and limiting factors. No one approach is likely to be appropriate all of the time. It is most important that middle managers are able to recognize what is getting in the way of results. This can sometimes be a challenge and may require that a middle manager use more than one model, or way of looking at how the work gets done. Here is a sampling of approaches and the eleven most common types of problems facing throughput:

Problem #1: Bottlenecks

A bottleneck is a point of congestion that reduces the flow of work and hinders progress and productivity. One way to recognize a bottleneck is by the work that piles up before the bottleneck and the people or process steps that are waiting for work coming from the bottleneck. There may be more than one bottleneck in a workflow or process. **FIGURE 8.1** shows a simple process. Steps B and C are bottlenecks because they can process less work than steps A and D do. If A consistently pushes at a rate of 25 per day and B at a rate of 20, work will pile up before steps B and C, and step D will be sometimes idle or pulling on step C for more work.

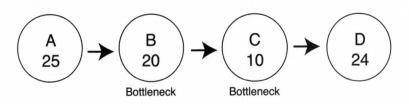

Fig. 8.1—A simple process with two bottlenecks

FIGURE 8.2 shows another common situation that produces bottlenecks. In this example, three separate processes all use the same resource, step C/L/S. A resource can be a person, a process step, a piece of machinery, or a computer function. This resource can handle the workload of any one process, but not all three. Step C/L/S is a major bottleneck. Steps J, K, B, and Q are also bottlenecks.

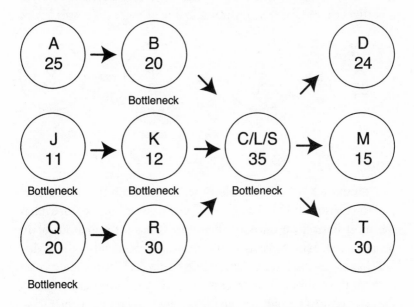

Fig. 8.2—Three processes with a common bottleneck

The story about Marty at the beginning of this chapter is an example of a bottleneck created when a resource serves multiple processes. Marty supported all processes in his department, but as a single resource he could not keep up with the demands from upstream and downstream customers and suppliers.

Problem #2: Constraints

A constraint is the bottleneck that has the most impact on overall throughput and results. There is only one constraint in a process or system. In fact, one constraint may affect several processes. A constraint can be a person, system, process step, piece of machinery, or computer function. In the previous example, Marty is a bottleneck and likely a constraint in one or more processes.

Fig. 8.3—A bottleneck and a constraint

FIGURE 8.3 shows a simple process with both the bottlenecks and the constraint identified. Step C is the constraint because it has the most impact on output. This process has a throughput of 10 because that is the capacity of the constraint. Remember the saying "A chain is only as strong as its weakest link?" The same logic holds true for throughput. The process step with the lowest capacity sets the pace of throughput. It is not always easy to find the constraint.

In **FIGURE 8.3**, the answer is simple. Looking at **FIGURE 8.2** again, it is not clear which step is the constraint. To decide this, the manager will need to calculate the time the C/L/S resource spends on each process vying for its time. If C = 10, L = 10, and S = 15, then this resource is the constraint for all three processes. If C = 23, L = 12, and S = 0, the C/L/S resource would be the constraint for the Q/R/S/T process (in fact, this process has stalled) but not for the other two processes. In this case, step B and step J are the constraints. If Marty is the C/L/S resource, it would help to identify how he spends his time and how his choices are affecting each project or process that relies on him. It is common for middle managers to spread their time evenly and become a bottleneck or constraint in many work processes or to focus on one or two projects and become the constraint on others. Neither of these approaches maximizes throughput.

Problem #3: Slow process connections

Sometimes the connections between resources affect throughput more than the process steps themselves do. This is particularly a problem with work processes that rely on two or more handoffs between people in the same or different departments. **FIGURE 8.4** shows a three-step process with two handoffs.

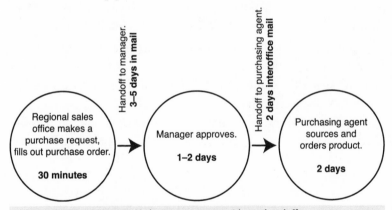

Fig. 8.4—A three-step process with two handoffs

The process steps to make a purchase add up to a total time of three to four days. However the total order processing time is much longer, as much as eight to twelve days, or up to three times longer! Process connections can often account for as much or more of the total throughput time as the process steps do. It is common for work to sit and wait for the next person or process step to move it forward. Much of the time spent between process steps is a waste of time and is a common cause of reduced throughput. Processes with many steps are particularly vulnerable to the effects of slow process connections. It is important to define the time used by process connections and process steps because the methods for improving throughput are different depending on where the inefficiencies lie.

Problem #4: Lengthy or complicated critical paths

A critical path shows the minimum amount of time a process or project will take to complete by identifying interdependent steps. Dependencies among steps slow processes. For example, if new computers cannot be purchased until the capital budget is approved, the work on installing new computers is dependent on the budget approval and the time it will take to complete the project needs to take this into account. Some work can occur concurrently, while other work depends on completion of a previous step. A critical path shows middle managers which interdependencies are affecting the overall throughput rate.

FIGURE 8.5 shows a simple critical path. In this example, the minimum critical path is six weeks and four days long. In other

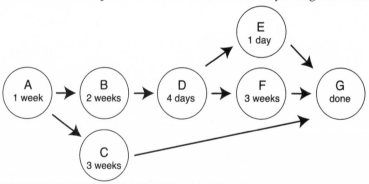

Fig. 8.5—A simple critical path

words, if everything goes well, and assuming the process connections are efficient, the work will take no less than six weeks and four days. Steps A, B, D, and F are on the critical path. They set the pace of results because of their dependency on each other. Step B cannot begin until step A is complete. Step F cannot begin until step D is complete, but can begin concurrently with step E. Step C can begin after step A but then does not impact other steps.

Remember Corky from earlier in the chapter? She needed to improve the speed and efficiency of the hiring process. It is likely that the process suffered from a long critical path and that Corky would have to change this to make any real improvements to hiring throughput. **FIGURE 8.6** on the following page illustrates what her hiring process looked like.

The critical path for the hiring process is a minimum of twenty-four days long! This assumes there is a steady stream of applications and that the recruiter does not need to advertise for the position. If there are not enough applicants, the hiring process is thirty to thirty-five days long. Given that most employees provide only a two-week notice before leaving the company, it is difficult for Corky's team to meet the organization's needs. The critical path for her hiring process was too long and did not serve her goal to have new employees in place when needed.

Problem #5: Skills deficiencies

One of the more common reasons for slower throughput of general work assignments and projects is a middle manager's inability to plan, monitor, and assign work. When middle managers have not learned the skills needed to organize and prioritize work, they put off the wrong tasks and waste time fighting preventable fires.

Paul did not plan well and this got in the way of his success. He worked hard and cared about the quality and success of his team.

What Paul could not see was that his inability to make better time-management choices hurt his department and his career. He had a long to-do list but failed to realize that all of his tasks were not equal.

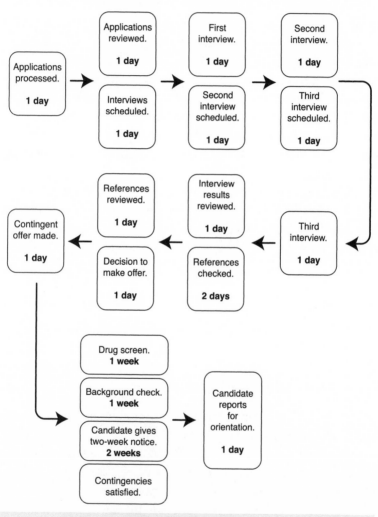

Fig. 8.6—Corky's hiring process

He did not have the experience or know-how to recognize important critical paths. To start the new season off well, he needed to be planning and making several important decisions six months in advance.

Instead, Paul spent his time on what was most pressing in his mind, which was work on a project due in a month. That work was important too, but Paul could have delegated it or delayed working on it for a week or two. Paul needed to do the departmental plan; however, by the time he got around to thinking about it, several important deadlines had passed. Inexperienced middle managers, like Paul, often do not feel a sense of urgency when it comes to planning and do not understand that the lead time needed for planning is just as important a deadline as other pressing tasks. Middle managers need to be excellent planners and communicators to ensure the work keeps flowing.

Other skills shortages get in the way of throughput as well. Middle managers who have not developed their abilities to partner, manage performance, set goals, or coach others will also suffer from lower throughput. Other chapters of this book address these skills.

Problem #6: Breakdowns

Breakdowns are system or process failures. People can also be the cause of breakdowns. Personal illnesses, vacations, and other situations that cause a person to stop working on a task could be considered breakdowns. When Tim first looked at the throughput in his department, he found that excessive use of sick days by several of his staff members caused lower productivity and work quality.

Problem #7: Errors

Errors are mistakes that cause rework or other additional work. The accounting department spent an average of six person-hours per week fixing accounts payable check run errors, or 5 percent of the team's total time at work! With a group of just three employees, this represents a significant waste of resources and a negative impact on their throughput.

Problem #8: Waste

Waste, as it relates to throughput, is work that is substandard or not usable, or work that, while satisfactory, is not used. When an employee copies and then distributes reports that few read, this is waste. The reports are usable, but few people are using them. It is also considered waste when marketing materials are scrapped due to inaccurate information. Waste uses resources that could otherwise be used for work that makes a difference. Waste reduces throughput potential. Reducing waste can be an easy and effective way to boost throughput without adding cost or resources.

Problem #9: Changes

Changes affect throughput in a variety of ways. When changes occur, error rates and waste may also increase. In addition, many changes result in temporary skills deficiencies and work-pace slow-downs. Middle managers should take into account the potential impact that changes will have on throughput. While some temporary productivity dips may be acceptable, a good middle manager should have some strategies in place for minimizing disruption.

Problem #10: Employee turnover

Employee turnover results in skills deficiencies, higher error rates, slower work pace, breakdowns, and waste. Throughput is often disrupted when employees leave.

Problem #11: Inadequate worker training

When changes and improvements are made, workers need to be retrained. Some skills are specialized enough that refresher training will improve throughput. When workers do not have the right training, they cannot do their best work.

Is it any wonder that a middle manager's job is so tough? Many things affect throughput. One of your most challenging and important responsibilities as a middle manager is to do whatever is necessary to diagnose and solve these problems to improve results.

Becoming Unstoppable—H.I.M.M. Techniques for Improving Throughput

High impact middle managers know how to zero in on problems affecting throughput. They focus on the areas posing the most significant challenges and systematically remove them or lessen their effect. The following techniques facilitate maximizing throughput and results when practiced regularly:

- Establishing a results-oriented environment
- Diagnosing throughput problems
- Solving throughput problems
- Asking the right questions

Establishing a Results-Oriented Environment

Middle managers who create work environments in which their employees quickly identify, openly discuss, and creatively solve problems will outproduce managers who do not. Managers cannot realistically expect to discover and tackle each problem themselves. When teams work together to ensure that nothing gets in the way of throughput, work is more productive and satisfying. Managers will know when this environment exists because improvements and problem solving happen naturally.

To create a results-oriented environment, middle managers should react positively and supportively to employees who bring problems to their attention. Do your employees feel comfortable discussing problems or errors? Do they feel sure that you care and want to know about the good, the bad, and the ugly? Do you provide negative reinforcement for raising questions or challenging ideas? Do your employees feel appreciated for their efforts to solve problems?

Middle managers who want to create a results-oriented work environment should be sure that they are accessible and responsive. Having regular and informal conversations with team members

CASE STUDY

Harry's employees did not share their ideas with him very often. Harry's first and most natural response was to be defensive. Even when his staff was not laying blame in Harry's direction, it seemed as though he took almost any concern, criticism, or alternative idea as personal censure. Harry also had the tendency to want to cover up problems in his area. Once, he had several managers who were bottlenecks to an important change the company was making. Instead of being open about this problem, Harry led senior management to believe that these managers backed the change effort and that there would be no problems with the implementation. When the senior managers later found out about the resistance, Harry said that he did not know it existed—even though his staff had told him about it weeks earlier. Harry gave his managers no reason to be proactive in identifying and communicating problems or barriers. As a result, they were reactive and their throughput suffered.

provides an opportunity for sharing news about the work. Managers who ask open-ended questions rooted in curiosity and support (versus those rooted in control) will discover people's concerns and ideas. Practicing MBWA daily helps middle managers stay in tune with daily happenings. These social activities serve a practical purpose. Managers who know what is going on in their department can better react to areas that need their time and support. Managers who routinely close their office doors or are inaccessible are not using one of the most valuable management tools to improve throughput: communication.

Diagnosing Throughput Problems

There are many possible reactions to barriers or problems affecting throughput. Deciding which actions will provide the greatest benefit requires analysis and diagnosis. The 80/20 rule applies here. One or a few remedies (20 percent) will have a more significant impact on results (80 percent) than most other possible actions. Your goal is to determine which responses will have the maximum benefit. To do this, it is important to classify the type of limitations getting in the way of throughput. The questions on the following page can help you decide how to focus your improvement efforts. Ask these questions with a process, system, or project in mind that is not experiencing satisfactory throughput.

For questions where the answer is unknown, take a moment to analyze and discover the answer. Taking the time to draw a diagram of the process or workflow can be enlightening. Middle managers can draw almost any work process or project using circles and arrows, as pictured earlier in this chapter. Be sure to define each process connection, as these handoffs are often a source of waste. Notice where the bottlenecks and the single step or person that is

Question	YES	NO	Priority
Is this process, system, or project plagued by bottlenecks?			
Is there more than one identifiable bottleneck?			
Is there one step, person, or part of the process that is holding up progress and forward movement of the work?			
Can you identify the constraint, or pacesetter?			
Is there a large difference between how long the work takes at each step and the total time of completion?			
Do handoffs between process or project steps take longer than wanted?			
Is the critical path too long?			
Are there opportunities to look at reducing dependencies between steps or tasks?			
Is the manager struggling to stay on top of the demands on his or her time?			
Does the manager lack practical experience or training in how to plan and communicate work?			
Is mucky muck a major problem impacting productivity?			
Have there been any breakdowns or shutdowns that affected this work?			
Is this process, project, or system plagued by errors?			
Does this process, system, or project waste time, energy, or resources?			
Has change negatively impacted the work?			
Has the team working on this process, project, or system suffered from turnover of personnel?			
Do any team members lack the needed skills to keep the work flowing?			

the constraint are. What is the pace of the constraint? If the pace is acceptable, then bottlenecks and constraints are not your primary problem. Next, try to create the critical path. When first defining a critical path, it is often surprising how many steps a process contains and how long the critical path is.

Each yes response in the worksheet suggests a possible focus for improvement. Once completed, the worksheet will help you evaluate various possible opportunities to improve throughput. Specific techniques that address areas of opportunity follow. After reviewing these suggestions, you will be able to determine which improvements will have the highest impact on results.

Eli Goldratt's Theory of Constraints

>>>   Author, scientist, and educator Eli Goldratt has advanced the science and practice of understanding throughput, constraints, and bottlenecks. In his books *The Goal, It's Not Luck,* and *Critical Chain,* Mr. Goldratt shares his theory of constraints (TOC) in a way that is helpful to middle managers who want to improve their results. Middle managers who oversee numerous or major processes or projects will benefit from reading Mr. Goldratt's books and learning about his TOC. This book does not seek to teach or explain TOC; rather, it is a general introduction for middle managers on various approaches to diagnosing and solving problems with throughput. Middle managers can find other resources on his Web site, *www.toc-goldratt.com.*

Solving Throughput Problems

Once a source for the throughput problem has been identified, middle managers should focus improvement efforts on finding a solution that will most improve results. For the best results and whenever possible, you should involve team members and peers in defining and implementing each solution. Involving others will improve commitment and accuracy and will speed up the implementation of changes.

Solution #1: Distinguish constraints from bottlenecks.

Middle managers may waste time removing bottlenecks that are not constraints. Individuals, teams, or departments who seek to optimize their part of a process without looking at the whole picture are most likely to face this problem. Here is a simple process with both the bottlenecks and the constraint identified.

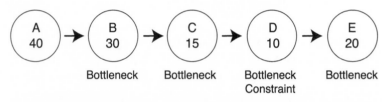

Fig. 8.7—A process with four bottlenecks and one constraint

In this process, B, C, D, and E are bottlenecks and D is the constraint. Work will pile up waiting for steps B and C to be completed and a huge pileup will accumulate before step D. The people or machines doing step E will sit idle if not utilized in other processes or projects.

Until D's performance improves, the overall process will produce at an approximate pace of 10. If this were a process contained within one team, it would be obvious that step D should be the starting point for improvement. But what if this process spanned several departments? In this case, you would need to work together to identify the constraint and concentrate on improving performance. This example is a simple one, but middle managers can look at and analyze any work process or project in the same way. Understanding both bottlenecks and the constraint will give you a better picture of the potential options for improving throughput. Using the process depicted in **FIGURE 8.7,** for example, the following questions might come to mind:

- What actions will improve step D's performance?
- Is there another resource, person, system, or machine that can take some of D's workload?
- What can the other process steps do to make step D's job easier and more efficient?
- Can steps A, B, and E provide resources to another process to improve its throughput?
- What throughput pace is acceptable? How can the workflow be optimized to enable the team to produce consistently at this pace?

Middle managers who take the time to identify and understand bottlenecks and constraints will have a valuable tool for improving results. Focusing on constraint performance will ensure that time and resources have the highest benefit.

Solution #2: Reduce the impact of constraints.

Once you identify a constraint, you can work to improve or supplement the constraint's performance. This is often the most valuable work that a middle manager can do, making this work a priority on the 80/20 list (the 20 percent of effort that produces 80 percent of results).When dealing with constraints, consider using the following steps:

1 › Test to ensure proper identification of the constraint. Constraints may be obvious or difficult to identify. To make sure that you identify the constraint correctly, ask yourself whether improving this process step would result in improvements to throughput. If the answer is yes, then it is more than likely that this resource is the constraint.

2 › Determine the potential capacity of the constraint. The constraint capacity is the amount of work, relating to a particular process, that can possibly be done under the best of circumstances. Middle managers need to be cautious not to consider a resource's total capacity when evaluating a constraint if the resource serves multiple processes or projects.

3 › Identify ways to improve capacity. Is it possible to improve the capacity of a resource? Sometimes yes, sometimes no. Simplification, automation, and upgrading abilities or skills are a few ways to improve the capacity of a resource.

4 › Identify additional resources to help lessen the constraint. Sometimes a resource needs to be augmented in order to improve throughput. When the constraint is a person, you, as a middle manager, will want to look at delegating work away from the constraint and rebalancing the workload. When the constraint is a system step, augmenting performance means adding components or diverting work to another part of the process.

5 › Optimize the efficiency of the constraint through better setups and handoffs. Middle managers may be able to improve the throughput of the constraint by changing the way work gets to and leaves this resource. If the process step preceding the constraint has excess capacity (relative to the pace of the constraint), having it take extra time to better prepare the work going to the constraint will be time well spent. Can you or a team member more effectively organize, document, or communicate the work before it gets to the constraint? Can the upstream resource queue up the work more effectively? Is the slowest person or machine spending time doing work that people or machines before or after it can perform?

Solution #3: Reduce bottlenecks when necessary.

There are at least two situations in which you as a middle manager will want to focus on improving bottlenecks to throughput. First, you need to address bottlenecks that are likely to become the next constraint, especially if the current constraint is already a focus for improvement. Second, you will want to improve bottlenecks as part of an overall process redesign or optimization. Improving bottleneck performance may allow it to augment the constraint's performance or become a resource for other processes. Here are some steps you can take:

1 > Test to ensure that improving this bottleneck will improve results. Before you spend time and energy on improving the performance of a bottleneck, you should assess whether the effort will make enough of a difference to warrant investment. Will this improvement pass the 80/20 test?

2 > Determine the bottleneck's capacity. How much high-quality work can this resource complete? Can this resource produce more?

3 > Identify ways to improve capacity. Is the employee or process efficient? Are all elements of the work necessary? Is there an opportunity to automate or combine steps?

4 > Identify additional resources to decrease the effect of bottlenecks. As they do when trying to improve constraint performance, middle managers should utilize other resources to help improve the overall performance of a process or project. Those who develop their skills in workload balancing will find they have more choices for improving throughput.

5 > Optimize the efficiency of the bottleneck through better setups and handoffs. It is important to ensure that work arrives at bottlenecks quickly and efficiently. If team members need to look up information or get an excessive number of approvals before beginning the work, their output will suffer. Bureaucracy and red tape often get in the way of progress and slow down results, particularly when they impact a constraint or bottleneck.

Solution #4: Shorten critical paths.

Many throughput problems occur because the process or project design does not support the needed pace of throughput. Middle managers often underestimate the time needed to get through the various parts of a process, or critical path. Corky's hiring process was an example of this. She thought that candidates should be able to get through the hiring process in a week in addition to the two weeks' notice the candidate would need to give to the current employer—in other words, a total of nineteen days. The critical path for the hiring process, however, was a minimum of twenty-four days long. Middle managers who take time to understand and improve the critical path of important work processes will be in a better position to improve their team's throughput and results. Here are some steps you can take when dealing with critical paths:

1 › Ensure the critical path is accurate and complete; beware of hidden steps or delays! When determining a critical path, managers should consider each component of the work, including smaller or shorter steps like approvals, paperwork, mailing times, and vendor lead times. It is also dangerous to assume the best-case scenario for estimating a critical path. Getting a signature on paperwork could happen in just a few minutes, but is this typical?

2 › Test assumptions about each step on the critical path. If the critical path is unacceptably long, you, as a middle manager, can begin to shave time off by challenging the assumptions behind each step. Does the work need to take this long? Is every step necessary? Can process changes allow for more steps that are concurrent?

3 ❯ Identify ways to shorten each step on the critical path. Middle managers can make tasks more efficient by considering alternative ways of doing the work. Can team members transmit, communicate, and share information electronically? Which tasks are candidates for automation? Can team members reduce specific parts of the work and still produce high-quality results?

4 ❯ Identify ways to shorten handoff times. The critical-path length may double when it includes the time needed for handoffs. The handoff, or process connection, often does not add any value to the work other than to facilitate communication and understanding. Reducing handoff times can be a quick and easy way to improve throughput. To reduce process-connection delays, middle managers must first define them and objectively determine their length or time. Managers can then reduce the number of process connections by challenging the use of each handoff. Eliminate needless handoffs. For cross-functional processes, it may be necessary to collaborate with peers to diagnose the root causes of slow process connections and to seek alternative approaches.

5 ❯ Reduce unnecessary steps. Most processes, particularly everyday work processes, have unnecessary steps. Identifying and eliminating unnecessary steps is the "low-hanging fruit" of process improvement. It is quick and effective but can occur only when middle managers analyze and evaluate work processes.

6 ❯ Determine methods for doing more work concurrently, but ensure that doing so will improve throughput. The more interdependent steps in the work process are, the longer the critical path will be. To support an environment where team members can work on many tasks at the same time, middle managers must communicate the work's status and progress more often and fully.

Solution #5: Improve skills.

Training and development are useful managerial tools for improving throughput. Both you and your team members need to ensure that you have the skills needed to complete the work quickly and well. It can be difficult for middle managers to evaluate their own development needs, but it becomes easier when the focus is on results and throughput. Are you getting projects completed on time? Do you wish results were better? With what tasks do you struggle? Are you able to complete the analytical work needed to solve throughput problems? Are you able to plan well? The answers to these and other questions may help you determine new skills that could benefit your team.

1 › Objectively determine needed skills. To maximize throughput, middle managers need to be excellent analyzers, planners, and communicators. The most common middle management development needs are planning and organizing work. These skills are also critical for improving throughput. Middle managers who struggle with deadlines and seem disorganized may need help and development in these areas. If your team members are unclear about their priorities and work assignments, then you definitely need training in planning and organizing work. For team members, time management and problem identification are often skills that need improvement. Specific technical skills may also help the manager and his or her team members work more effectively.

2 › Identify learning resources. Who in the organization is strong in the area needing development? Can they mentor an employee needing development? What training options will work the best in this case? Search for recent books, tapes, and articles on the topic. For middle managers who need to develop their ability to plan and analyze work, there are, unfortunately, fewer choices. Finding a mentor or coach within or outside the organization will probably be the best solution for developing these important skills.

3 > Establish learning follow-up and reinforcement. Middle managers who take the time and energy to develop themselves and team members should also invest in follow-up and reinforcement of these newly developed skills. The best way to reinforce learning is to use the new skills! If team members have attended training, make sure to utilize the new skills. This will benefit the team and provide them with work that is likely to be intrinsically motivating.

Solution #6: Deal with other barriers to throughput.

Barriers to throughput challenge middle managers regularly. The following general skills for diagnosing and solving problems will be invaluable tools for dealing with most of these challenges.

1 > Diagnose the root cause of problems affecting throughput. Middle managers who ask why problems occur until they get to the root cause of an issue will be in a better position to affect real and lasting improvements. To diagnose the root causes of problems, excellent collaboration skills and a healthy sense of curiosity are important. Review each of the potential problems affecting throughput presented earlier in this chapter. Ask peers and team members for input. Test ideas and assumptions to determine if they are valid.

2 > Notice and address patterns, themes, and recurring barriers. Many problems happen repeatedly and may go unnoticed for some time. Often, the only way to understand and see the problem is to notice the patterns of difficulty or recurring smaller issues. Is there a theme or pattern that could shed light on the underlying problem with a process or project?

3 **>**   Become a barrier obliterator. Middle managers who make it a mission to seek out and destroy barriers to throughput will improve results more quickly and completely than those who do not. Being proactive or reacting quickly is better than waiting until results deteriorate to respond. Middle managers lose precious time when they do not address emerging problems. High impact middle managers often think about the things getting in the way of throughput and then they take action to improve results.

The Most Important Question Middle Managers Should Ask

Middle managers who want to improve throughput should always ask the following question: "What are the one or two changes that will have the most impact on the overall throughput of this work?" Said another way, the question becomes, "What is the 20 percent that will improve throughput by 80 percent?" Whether the focus is on the constraint, bottlenecks, critical paths, connections, skills, mucky muck, or other barriers, the question is the same. A few improvements can have a significant and positive impact on results.

It is not always easy to discern the changes that will have a significant impact from those that will not make much of a difference. To ensure that you have determined the best changes to make, ensure that adequate analysis and testing has been done. In addition, the impact previous changes have made should be assessed and considered. Do not make the same or similar mistakes repeatedly. Once your team implements the modification, they should closely monitor throughput to evaluate the effect the change is having.

Chapter 9

Using H.I.M.M. to Make the Most of Your Busy Day

JIM FELT DISCOURAGED about how little he accomplished at work. Every day was an exercise in frustration, playing catch-up, and rolling tasks onto tomorrow's "to-do" list. Jim always felt behind the curve—despite working long days and extra hours. He was not able to prioritize his schedule because everything seemed important, and he spent most of his day in meetings or talking with his managers. He knew that the ways in which he spent his time did not match up with the priorities and expectations that his manager had of him, but he still allowed himself to gravitate to doing the work that was most comfortable for him, rather than what needed to get done. While he talked a great deal about the importance of planning, he spent more time talking about planning than actually doing it. Jim used planners, to-do lists, and whiteboards but still felt like he was not on top of things. In addition, he stalled out when he was emotionally uncomfortable with a task or decision.

Jim is not alone. Many middle managers have more tasks on their to-do list than they can ever complete and they don't know what they can do to improve their situation. This state of affairs is endemic to middle management and will not go away by working two more hours each day. Working more is not the answer, and burnout is the likely result. To gain control, middle managers should examine how they are spending time and make choices that will yield better results.

Four Fallacies about Time

One of the barriers many middle managers face regarding their time is their perceptions about time management. How many times have you heard yourself, or a fellow middle manager, utter the following statements?

- There is never enough time!
- If it ain't broke, don't fix it.
- If it is worth doing, it's worth doing right.
- Slowing down decreases output.

If you are a busy middle manager who works too much (many middle managers fit into this group), the best solution to issues with time might be to change your beliefs about time and your definition of what successful use of your time looks like. These four fallacies about time illustrate ways in which beliefs can get in the way of good time management.

Fallacy #1: There is never enough time!

As managers get older and retire, they rarely think back and wish they had spent more time at the office. If anything, their sentiments are quite the opposite; many managers lament that they lost important parts of their lives by working too much. Time is a unit of life, a slice of one's experience here on Earth. A middle manager has over 10,000 minutes each week to divvy up for what's most meaningful, important, or fun to do. Those who regularly choose to work too many hours a week are shortchanging other parts of their life.

As a middle manager, making good choices about how to manage your time is not just a desirable thing to do; it is essential. Like a traffic cop in the middle of a busy intersection, middle managers need to make good decisions about which work moves forward and how quickly.

Managers who work more may produce less. This may sound counterintuitive, but managers who routinely work late or on weekends are not as productive or effective as those who spend fewer hours at work. Although you may work more than sixty hours a week, your number of truly productive hours is generally less than forty. At a certain point, the exhaustion of working sixty hours a week will yield diminishing returns in terms of loss of concentration, diminished creativity, and low morale. The way to become more successful is not to work harder, but to work smarter.

Mindy was a middle manager who worked too much. She was invited to take part in numerous meetings about all aspects of the company, and people valued her input and ideas. Mindy liked to participate, enjoyed knowing what was going on in the company, and had a hard time saying no. Because these meetings took up so much of her day, she worked evenings and weekends to get her other work done. She allowed herself to become the go-to person for more topics than was practical or efficient. She accepted, and sometimes encouraged, scope creep that broadened her job responsibilities to the point that she could do many things halfheartedly, but few well.

Deep down, Mindy knew this and was worried about it to the point that it took a toll on her health. When she was under pressure, she was jittery, had a nervous tic, and did not take the time to listen during conversations. She was present, but her mind was not with the conversation. This only exacerbated the problem. Mindy used her busy schedule as an excuse for not managing better. Senior management could see she was busy and working long hours and, as a result, let her poor performance slide. Over time, her managers' expectations fell. Her job suffered and she did not achieve the best results possible. Her life was out of balance.

Jane's story was different but no more effective. In addition to spreading herself too thin and getting involved in too many tasks, Jane puttered her time away. She worked numerous hours, but many of them were spent on unimportant tasks. She did not know how to prioritize, plan, or execute work, and did nothing to ensure her team was working on the right action plans. As a result, she and her department spent their time on tasks that made little difference within the company.

Jane allowed herself to spend several hours a day responding to routine requests and inquiries. A better use of her time would have been to build the independence and capacity of her organization so each of her team members could address and solve many of the daily issues. Jane focused on the tyranny of the urgent rather than on what was valuable. Jane also procrastinated to the last possible moment, then came in on the evenings and weekends to get the work done on time, or at least not too late. However, she never left enough time, so her work was often poorly done and incomplete. Jane had more than enough time to get her job done but wasted most of it.

Jim, Mindy, and Jane would probably all say that if they only had more time, they could be more successful. The fact is that, even if they had more time, their poor time-management habits would get in the way and they would end up producing the same unsatisfactory results. They did not need more time; they needed to spend their time more productively. Until middle managers are using their forty hours a week optimally, they should resist the temptation to work more hours and throw the rest of their life out of balance.

Fallacy #2: If it ain't broke, don't fix it.

One of the greatest wastes of time in corporate America is continuing to do things the same way because it seems to be working. Often, middle managers do not even know if their processes, systems, or practices are serving the outcome because they have not recently evaluated them. Sticking with the status quo may not save time and is more likely to waste it. What if there was a better way to do the work? Have the conditions that justified the current approach changed? What if the goals have changed but the work has not?

As the primary change agent within your company, you, as a middle manager, need to question the status quo and ensure that processes and practices are set up to deliver the desired results. When goals change, practices and processes must also change. Hesitating or failing to change ideas or approaches that are comfortable wastes time and money. (Techniques for improving processes can be found in this chapter as well as in Chapter 7.)

Jake told his middle managers that he wanted them to improve their analysis capabilities so they could make better decisions. The end goal was to increase productivity, quality, and profitability throughout the organization. It was a great strategy but it proved hard to achieve. Jake and many of the other middle managers assumed that the goal of greater accountability and ownership could happen within their current business practices. They were wrong. As things stood, many of their company's processes and systems did not support the type of functional analysis and optimization that Jake and the other managers wanted to implement. Middle managers could not get the data they needed to make sound judgments. In addition, team members did not know how to, or buy into why they should, spend more time measuring their effectiveness. Comfort with the status quo was getting in the way and wasting time. To improve the business, they needed to question whether their current processes and systems were satisfactory or needed to change.

Fallacy #3: If it's worth doing, it's worth doing right.

The problem with this statement comes from how middle managers define "doing things right." If the standard for "right" is perfect or restrictive, then waiting to do things right could lead to procrastination, inaction, and bottlenecks. Of course, high-quality work is important and always the goal, but if you wait to do things until conditions are perfect, you will produce less and miss important opportunities.

Bob fell into this time trap a lot. He procrastinated because he wanted to wait until he had enough time to focus on the problem or opportunity. Guess what? He *never* had enough time—and was never going to. Bob missed several opportunities because he was simply too picky and slow. Why did he do this? In Bob's case, he felt that if he were not perfect, his customers would not value him. While his internal and external customers wanted quality work, what they missed most from Bob and his team were action and results.

Lonny knew several members of his team were not performing adequately. Each time Lonny's manager talked to him about this, Lonny had another reason the time was not right to make the necessary changes. The busy season was coming up and he did not have time to train new employees. His team recently lost a member, so he couldn't afford to make other changes in personnel. The supervisor had changed and Lonny wanted to see if his employees might respond to this new person more favorably. And on, and on. Each excuse may have been valid, but together they formed a pattern of inaction and demonstrated Lonny's hesitancy to take care of the problem. The conditions were never going to be perfect for Lonny to take control of the situation and make the necessary changes. Eventually, Lonny was fired and replaced by a manager who was willing to be more proactive.

If you're one of those middle managers who has the tendency to wait too long to take action, a good mantra might be Shakespeare's famous quote, "He who hesitates is lost." Waiting until the timing is just right wastes time and slows down progress.

Fallacy #4: Slowing down decreases output.

In some cases, going slow is the best way to go faster. Ready, aim, fire. Slow, slow, fast. To achieve excellent results, it is best to complete a methodical up-front analysis (slow), plan well (slow), and energetically implement (fast). Middle managers who spend more time on up-front planning and ensuring that the work supports their goals will outpace and outperform those who rush things. In addition, pausing midstream to analyze how the work is going can create much-needed energy to move the work forward or facilitate a breakthrough.

At Black & Decker, one of the key factors that enabled the team to reduce the product development cycle for the DeWalt power tool line was investing more time up-front. Black & Decker devoted more time to ensuring they knew the features and benefits each tool should have, and then to designing the tool for the highest quality and manufacturability. They also took time to do some team training and role clarification that improved productivity and communication during the project-management phase. Because of the time allocated up-front, they were able to shorten the product development cycle by months.

Be aware, however, that sometimes being slow is just slow. The activities that take time up-front but pay off in the end include good analysis, effective planning, clarifying expectations and roles, and relationship building. Middle managers who spend more time doing these things will find that their throughput improves.

Letting Go of the Victim Mentality

The previous four fallacies about time obstruct middle managers from making the most of their day. Another significant barrier that reduces your effectiveness is victim conversations about time. A victim conversation is something you say or think that has a "woe is me" quality to it. When it comes to time, a victim conversation might sound like this:

- "I am so busy, I can't think straight."
- "I don't have time for this."
- "Another day is gone and I didn't even put a dent in my to-do list."

Debbie, a middle manager at a *Fortune* 500 company, was a big whiner when it came to time. Although she had a huge job and many time-related challenges, her victim conversations got in her way more than all the other challenges put together. Her victim conversations kept her from taking action and stopped her from thinking creatively. When Debbie thought or spoke about her frustrations with time, in that moment, she made it impossible for herself to progress. Think about how ridiculous these complaints sound:

> "I can't believe the day is already half over. I have not sat at my desk for five minutes all day. I do not know when I am going to be able to get all of this done. I would not wish this job on my enemy."

How can anything productive follow statements like those? When people like Debbie habitually gripe about not having time, they are sealing their fate and making their problem worse. Venting frustrations now and then is natural, but when it is a common response, the victim conversation becomes a major barrier to success.

H.I.M.M. Techniques for Mastering Time

High impact middle managers have beaten the time demons and learned to make wise choices about how to spend their day. They know that managing time well will enable them to work more on meaningful projects and establish a better work/life balance, which is needed to stay sane and happy. The H.I.M.M. techniques for mastering time include the following:

- Perform periodic time audits.
- Set the pace.
- Apply the 80/20 rule to choices about time.
- Use tiny pockets of time to get big results.
- Plan, plan, plan.

In addition, these managers have come to know that their good time-management habits have rubbed off on their team members. High impact middle managers lead by example.

Technique #1: Perform periodic time audits.

The best way for middle managers to determine how efficiently they use time is to complete a time audit. A time audit reveals the level of alignment that exists between the middle manager's goals and how he or she spends time. Unlike other time inventories, the time audit does not seek to detail how a manager spends each minute. The time audit focuses on the type of activity, not each specific action. Not only would it take too much time to complete a detailed inventory, but it is also unnecessary. To perform a time audit, you need to complete the exercise on the following page.

Time Audit	
Part 1:	*RESPONSE*
My broad goals, based on my manager's expectations, are . . .	
My most important priorities are . . .	
I am most concerned about . . .	
The barriers getting in the way of my team's productivity are . . .	
Planning and analysis that I need to complete in the next month include . . .	
Part 2:	*RESPONSE*
The approximate percentage of my time spent on items described in part 1 has been . . .	
Are the actions I am taking adding value?	
Average number of hours a week I have spent in meetings is . . .	
Are these meetings a good use of my time? Why/why not?	
Which meetings should I keep and which should I no longer go to?	
Are the meetings well run and effective?	
How successful are my employees? What have I done to optimize their performance?	
How clear is my team about what's expected of them and which tasks are of highest priority? When was the last time I talked to them about this?	

》》》

Time Audit (continued)	
Part 2: (continued)	*RESPONSE*
If I were to share how I spent my time today with the CEO, my manager, my peers, and my employees, what would they likely say?	
How much time over the past week did I spend doing versus managing?	
How many hours do I work on average?	
Part 3	*RESPONSE*
Based on this time audit, what goals should I set to improve the ways in which I spend time?	
What beliefs should I take on to help support these goals?	
What immediate actions can I take to begin using time more wisely?	

The time audit emphasizes the things that are most important for a middle manager to devote his or her time to. Here, again, is the form, with comments about how to interpret responses.

Time Audit	
Part 1:	*RESPONSE*
My broad goals, based on my manager's expectations, are . . .	*Part 1 is a place to establish what the priorities should be. It is important to take the time to fill out this section so the answers can be referred to during the other parts of the audit. In addition, the act of summarizing the priorities will help middle managers focus on them.*
My most important priorities are . . .	
I am most concerned about . . .	
The barriers getting in the way of my team's productivity are . . .	
Planning and analysis that I need to complete in the next month include . . .	

Time Audit *(continued)*	
Part 2:	*RESPONSE*
The approximate percentage of my time spent on items described in part 1 has been . . .	*Middle managers should spend at least 75 percent of their time, or six hours a day, on the work described in part 1.*
Are the actions I am taking adding value?	*It is important to make sure the actions are not only aligned to goals, but that the action is the best choice out of many possible actions. For example, asking a peer about a concern may support resolving the concern, but is this action going to make a difference? Would calling a meeting and brainstorming potential solutions be a better use of the same time?*
Average number of hours a week I have spent in meetings is . . .	*Middle managers tend to spend too much time in meetings. It is valuable to question the meetings attended and their effectiveness. If a meeting is not effective, ask the meeting leader to make positive changes or stop attending, if possible.*
Are these meetings a good use of my time? Why/why not?	
Which meetings should I keep and which should I no longer go to?	
Are the meetings well run and effective?	
How successful are my employees? What have I done to optimize their performance?	*Middle managers need to focus on enabling their employees to perform their best. Many busy middle managers allow their attention to get diverted by the needs of the day and may go months without thinking about how to coach and facilitate performance. Ideally, optimizing individual and team performance was identified in part 1 as a top priority. If not, it should be added.*
How clear is my team about what's expected of them and which tasks are of highest priority? When was the last time I talked to them about this?	
If I were to share how I spent my time today with the CEO, my manager, my peers, and my employees, what would they likely say?	*Middle managers should be able to answer this question. The answer might differ depending on the audience. Overall, middle managers should be able to gain support and agreement that they are working on the tasks that are important and beneficial.*

»»

Time Audit *(continued)*	
Part 2: *(continued)*	**RESPONSE**
How much time over the past week did I spend doing versus managing?	*Depending on the specifics of each middle manager's job, this number will vary. It is important to notice whether doing gets more attention than managing and why. Is it because doing is more comfortable and satisfying?*
How many hours do I work on average?	*Middle managers who work more than forty hours per week on average should look at how they spend their time and ensure that they get the most value out of each hour worked. Managers who work more than sixty hours per week are not managing their time well and should seek to reduce the number of hours worked while improving productivity.*
Part 3	**RESPONSE**
Based on this time audit, what goals should I set to improve the ways in which I spend time?	*Summarize revelations, ideas, and conclusions here.*
What beliefs should I take on to help support these goals?	*Beliefs might include statements like, "As a middle manager, I am expected to optimize individual and team performance and I need to be spending more time focusing on this to meet this expectation and responsibility." Or, "Right now, the top priority is planning for the coming busy season. Time spent working on this now will benefit my team and me later. I need to make sure that nothing gets in the way of this important planning."*
What immediate actions can I take to begin using time more wisely?	*Be bold and assertive when making this list, because doing so will be more energizing and empowering. "I don't know" is not an acceptable answer. The list should contain at least ten possible actions.*

The time audit is useful for determining the alignment that exists between the ways in which a middle manager spends his or her time and the results that are most important. If you find you are spending too much time on tasks not listed in part 1, try to resist the urge to rationalize or make excuses. While it is true that most middle managers face dozens of requests a day for their time, it is your responsibility to determine the best method to get the work completed. Middle managers need to be able to decline requests that get in the way of work that should be their top priority.

Technique #2: Set the pace.

Middle managers determine the pace of the organization. Pace is the rate at which work proceeds. Pace is also the rate at which a person walks. For middle managers, both definitions are important. To establish and maintain an electric, exciting, and productive pace that feels good to work within, the pace of the work and the people needs to be brisk. In a work environment like this, workers feel like making things happen and they accomplish more. Intel and Amazon.com are examples of companies with a brisk pace; there is nothing lethargic about their work environments! People walk down the hallways with determination and speed. They are clearly thinking about something. Within earshot are two people engaged in a lively discussion about how to solve a problem. In a meeting room, a manager is drawing a diagram on the whiteboard, arrows going everywhere, heads nodding.

While both Intel and Amazon.com are high-tech companies and might be expected to have a fast-paced environment, that is not why their pace is fast. Their work pace is brisk because their middle managers make it so. Any workplace, even a 125-year-old paper mill, can have an exciting pace if the middle managers create that type of environment. Here's how to create pace:

- MBWA often. It does not do any good if you only leave your desk once a day. Managers who circulate and talk to their people, as well as other departments and managers, are informed, perceived as accessible, and create a positive energy in the office.
- Initiate action every day. Get moving on projects or ideas that are on the to-do list. Do not allow procrastination to get in the way of action.
- Facilitate meetings and ask people to participate (as opposed to meetings where the leader speaks and everyone else just sits there). Facilitate brainstorming or problem-solving sessions on a regular basis.
- Ask people for their ideas every day.
- Express a sense of urgency that comes from being excited about the work.
- Celebrate successes and create anticipation for future successes.
- Have fun at work. Smile and laugh. Take the work seriously, but enjoy it, too.
- Make the removal of barriers and mucky muck a top priority. Prevent anything from getting in the way of your team's progress.

Tim, a middle manager at a software company, was always on the move. Striding down the hallway, he looked like a man with a mission and purpose. Anyone could stop him, though, and strike up a conversation. Tim would jump into the conversation with fervor and interest. He always worked at a brisk pace and emitted a focused energy that rubbed off on others in his area. He would share at least one new idea daily. To his boss, Tim was a bit of a nuisance, but in a good way. His employees began thinking more quickly, too. Within three months, Tim had improved the pace of his new department through being an outstanding role model and encouraging a fun and lively work environment.

Technique #3: Apply the 80/20 rule to choices about time.

The time audit reveals whether you are spending your time on work that matters. As a middle manager you can use the 80/20 rule to help make wise choices about how you use your time. Of all the items on an average daily to-do list, there are 20 percent that are critical. This 20 percent produces 80 percent of the results. A high impact middle manager identifies and focuses on that 20 percent. When the fire drills of the day begin to usurp time, high impact middle managers prioritize the 20 percent that needs to remain the focus. If something in the schedule has to be cut, they make sure it's not part of that 20 percent.

CASE STUDY

Jim's responsibilities were undergoing a fundamental shift. Jim and his manager had agreed that Jim's top priority was to leverage signs of recovery in the market and focus on maximizing revenue for the company. Jim's job was to make sure that the company seized every available opportunity to increase revenues. Almost overnight, Jim's focus changed. No longer would he spend time on any topic of discussion; he began entrusting his most competent managers to handle more issues and decisions without him. He let staff know that he was going to back out of selected meetings and spend more time focusing on tasks that were aligned with his new mandate.

Jim's direct and forthcoming approach worked; his managers quickly adjusted to the level and type of involvement that was being asked of them. Jim learned that the best way to improve how he spent his time was to first make different and better choices, then clearly and openly communicate these changes to team members and peers. To keep himself on track, Jim would ask himself if the task he was working on was going to impact revenue. If not, he would delegate the task to focus his time on his most critical objective—generating revenue.

Sometimes middle managers think that if they work harder,

they will be able to accomplish their goals. Often, though, the most important choice they make is regarding *what* they will do, not how hard they will work. This point is illustrated well in the following short parable written by Ralph Stayer:

I'm sitting in a quiet room at the Millcroft Inn, a peaceful little place hidden back among the pine trees about an hour out of Toronto. It's just past noon, late July, and I'm listening to the desperate sounds of a life or death struggle going on a few feet away.

There's a small fly burning out the last of its short life's energies in a futile attempt to fly through the glass of the windowpane. The whining wings tell the poignant story of the fly's strategy—try harder.

But it's not working.

The frenzied effort offers no hope for survival. Ironically, the struggle is part of the trap. It is impossible for the fly to try hard enough to succeed at breaking through the glass. Nevertheless, this little insect has staked its life on reaching its goal through raw effort and determination.

The fly is doomed. It will die there on the windowsill.

Across the room, ten steps away, the door is open. Ten seconds of flying time and this small creature could reach the outside world it seeks. With only a fraction of the effort now being wasted, it could be free of this self-imposed trap. The breakthrough possibility is there. It would be so easy.

Why doesn't the fly try another approach, something dramatically different? How did it get so locked in on the idea that this particular route and determined effort offer the most promise for success? What logic is there in continuing until death, to seek a breakthrough with "more of the same"? No doubt, this approach makes sense to the fly. Regrettably, it's an idea that will kill.

Simply trying harder and harder is an approach that makes sense to many middle managers. Unfortunately, it often leads to burnout rather than success. Trying harder isn't necessarily the solution to achieving more. It may not offer any real promise for giving you what you want out of life. Sometimes, in fact, it's a big part of the problem. If you stake your hopes for a breakthrough on trying harder than ever, you may kill your chances for success.

Creating Work/Life Balance

>>> In his bestselling book *Maverick: The Success Story Behind the World's Most Unusual Workplace,* Ricardo Semler, the well-known and well-regarded CEO of Semco in Brazil, had this to say about the importance of handling time: "I took sixteen aspirins in just one day. Before I could reorganize Semco, I had to reorganize myself. Long hours were the first issue I tackled. They were one of the biggest symptoms of time sickness, a disease that afflicts far too many executives. So I set 7 P.M. as the time I would leave the office, no matter what. After that, I would go to the movies, read books (but not business books)—anything but work. I wouldn't do any work on the weekends, either. . . . Yes, I would attack my problem directly, and that problem was not simply the management of a business but something even more fundamental: the management of time."

Many managers suffer from what Semler calls time sickness. They equate quality with quantity and attack work backlogs with a try-harder mentality. This approach is a recipe for burnout and failure. High impact middle managers have learned that managing time enables many other successes to occur.

Technique #4: Use tiny pockets of time to get big results.

It is 8:53 A.M. and there is a meeting scheduled to begin at 9:00 A.M. Brett has prepared for the meeting and the needed materials are copied, organized, and ready to distribute. What should he do now? There isn't enough time to start anything new, or is there? Glancing quickly at his to-do list, Brett got up and sought out one of his employees. He asked a few questions, clarified what needed to occur, and asked the employee to follow up with peers in another department. Returning to his desk, he grabbed his materials, and several other items to drop off in the mailroom on the way to the meeting. In the hall outside the meeting, Brett chatted with a peer and resolved an open issue on his to-do list. He quickly lets his employees know so that they could immediately act on the information instead of waiting until the meeting was over. Brett was still among the first to arrive at the meeting and in seven minutes accomplished three tasks that helped his team members work more effectively.

High impact middle managers routinely use tiny pockets of time to accomplish tasks on their to-do lists. It's all too easy to waste the few minutes before meetings or appointments. Most people figure there is not enough time to start anything big, so why bother? There are two reasons using these small amounts of time wisely will pay off. First, and most obviously, middle managers who use this time wisely will get more work done. If the average middle manager has five segments in his or her day, and the manager completes a couple of tasks before each segment begins, that's ten additional tasks completed each day! Second, and just as important, doing things in these small bits of time energizes you and keeps you on pace. Conversely, wasting time scatters motivation and energy. Tasks that lend themselves to this practice include:

- Checking in with an employee
- Asking a peer for clarification
- Reading a quick article or memo
- Sharing information
- Requesting a report or information for analysis to be done later

- Returning a quick phone call
- Filling out paperwork that has been sitting in your in-box for too long
- Sending out a meeting appointment and creating the agenda
- MBWA

Middle managers can use tiny pockets of time to facilitate a breakthrough. Taking ten minutes to ask new, open-ended questions can spur fresh thinking on how to solve an old problem. It takes just a few moments to create and deliver several new questions verbally or by e-mail. If the questions help move the problem or project forward, these ten minutes may prove to be the most valuable time you spend all day.

Technique #5: Plan, plan, plan.

Most middle managers do not spend enough time planning. Often, they opt to deal with the tyranny of the urgent and let planning slide. This strategy is rarely effective because it begins a vicious

---

CASE STUDY

Todd was an excellent planner; fortunately, this skill rubbed off on his peers. In work sessions or meetings, Todd would frequently ask, "What's the plan?" or "Do we have a plan for how we are going to accomplish this?" He would ask questions that slowed the group down and made them focus on the tasks involved, each person's role in the project, and due dates. This process prevented Todd and his team from overcommitting. Todd knew that taking the time to talk through the planning for each major project would serve him and his colleagues well in the end. His excellent planning helped them execute tasks more effectively. Todd's work was never late. He managed his day to ensure that he completed the most important work first. When he committed to doing something, people knew they could count on Todd to deliver.

cycle of not spending time on the right tasks, because there is no good work plan, because there is no time to plan, and so on. Each day, middle managers should take a few minutes to plan their day. Weekly and monthly planning are equally as important. (Techniques for creating excellent work plans can be found in Chapter 7.)

Planning can be a therapeutic practice for middle managers who worry that there is too much to do. Concerns about remembering what is most important and what if something falls through the cracks are allayed when a good plan is in place. With a good work plan, you can breathe easier because the most important work will be at the top of the list. Even though a work plan may be daunting and contain a long list of tasks, having a plan is always more comforting than worrying about what-if scenarios.

Middle managers who do not make good choices about how to spend their time will likely suffer from career setbacks, a poor work/life balance, and suboptimal results. To the casual observer, they may appear scattered and overwhelmed. Conversely, those who ensure their time is focused on doing the right things in an efficient manner will experience more success and satisfaction. They will appear to be on top of things and confident. High impact middle managers have time to get their jobs done and be accessible and responsive to team members and peers. These effective managers periodically review how they are spending their time and ensure that they have their priorities straight. For the busy middle manager, time is a precious commodity that needs to be proactively and effectively utilized.

Part Four

**H.I.M.M. Performance Leadership—
Ensuring Team Members Excel in Execution**

Chapter 10

Performance Management Myths—
What Not to Do

MIKE COMPLAINED THAT he wasn't able to spend much time managing his people because he had too many other important tasks to do. He did not enjoy having performance conversations or team meetings and generally tried to avoid them. Meanwhile, his two teams were struggling with different performance challenges. One team employed many smart and hardworking people who were overwhelmed by ambiguous roles and turnover within the department. The other team lacked focus and had several people who were not a good fit for their respective positions. Both teams lacked effective and proactive management. Compounding the problem was the fact that many members of Mike's staff had become helpless while working for three ineffective managers over the last five years.

Mike found his team's performance unsatisfactory, but his assumptions about management were getting in the way of his correcting the problem. First, optimizing individual performance does not take much time. Mike spent more time than that reacting to problems that wouldn't have occurred if he had spent more time managing well from the beginning. Second, Mike's belief that managing performance was secondary to his other work handicapped his effectiveness. One of the most important contributions a middle manager can make is to ensure that his or her teams are performing well and getting results. Mike thought that if he ignored the problem long enough, it would either fix itself, go away, or become someone else's problem. Those beliefs were not helping Mike solve the performance problems within his teams. He needed to replace those management assumptions with more helpful ones.

H.I.M.M. helps middle managers optimize performance by clarifying which actions improve performance and which do not. H.I.M.M. then focuses on developing the skills needed to carry out the most worthwhile practices. As with many areas of management, the 80/20 rule applies. There are a few managerial habits (the 20 percent) that will make the greatest impact (the 80 percent) on individual performance. To get to the 20 percent, it is first important to understand the management assumptions that are not helpful and the actions that either work poorly or do not work at all (the 80 percent of actions that yield only 20 percent of results).

Five Myths about Managing People

At one time, many scientists thought the world was flat. Ten years ago, most people could not have conceived of using cell phones to take pictures and play games. The medical community is continually revising its list of foods that are healthful and those that are not. Each year, science and industry learn new and better ways to solve problems and get things done. Throughout the past fifty years, what is known and believed about management has been changing as well. The following five myths about managing people are examples of where research and experience indicate a change in perspectives and practices is warranted.

- Employees do not want management.
- Performance evaluation systems improve performance.
- Employees prefer a sugarcoated counseling session to a candid one.
- Positive reinforcement is a great tool for improving performance.
- Salary increases improve employee motivation and productivity.

Myth #1: Employees do not want management.

It might be true that employees dislike micromanagement, but it is not correct to assume that employees do not want to work in a well-managed department. Employees who work for poor managers often feel frustrated, lost, unfocused, and unsuccessful. They may even feel abandoned. Employees expect and hope that their manager will show leadership, plan the work, and make sure everyone

CASE STUDY

Jim terminated Jane because she did not manage well. Senior managers worried her employees would be angry and upset when they learned the news. Jane was fun, friendly, and well liked. Much to the senior managers' surprise, Jane's employees were not angry. Though they felt sad for Jane, they knew from firsthand experience that she was not a good functional manager and saw her departure as an opportunity to bolster the team's success. Jane's replacement experienced little resistance, and many employees asked why it took senior management so long to make the change.

is doing his or her job. They want their manager to ensure the team is working on the right tasks and is aware of changes that are happening within the department and the organization. Employees want to know whether their work is satisfactory, or if performance concerns exist, to be told about them honestly and in a timely fashion. If something is wrong, employees want their managers to have the courage and conviction to deal with it quickly. This includes dealing with nonperformers who are not pulling their weight. Employees do not respect managers who don't or won't manage.

Employees recognize that it is their manager's responsibility to be proactive and a leader in ensuring all members of the team are performing. Employees do not want to feel as though they are being managed in a controlling or dogmatic way, but good, effective functional management is both desired and expected.

Myth #2: Performance evaluation systems improve performance.

In his classic book *Out of the Crisis,* quality expert W. Edwards Deming called performance evaluation systems one of the deadly diseases of Western management. Alfie Kohn, a university professor and expert on human behavior, said in his book *Punished by Rewards,* "Even if performance appraisals were adequate to gauge how well people are doing, their effects are usually so destructive that they shouldn't be used anyway." Management and quality consultant Peter Scholtes had this to say in his article "Performance Without Appraisal": "For most people, either giving or receiving a performance appraisal is like a visit to the dentist: it is not fun, but it is good for you. Here is some news for you: performance appraisal is not good for you. Performance appraisal, when looked at more deeply, not only does no good, it does harm. Performance appraisal, in fact, is a flat-out disaster, a virus that is going to damage our organizations and our people. . . . Performance appraisal is an example of the old philosophy. It is a remnant of obsolescence which clings like a parasite, draining energy from our organizations." Management consultant and writer Peter Block shares his sentiment about performance appraisal: "Sold as a developmental experience, I think the real function of performance appraisal and its derivatives is more about maintaining control. It is a time, once a year, when we are reminded by our boss and the institution that they own us."

Performance evaluations do not improve performance. This may seem like a bizarre statement in light of the fact that almost every company uses an appraisal system to manage performance. Could all these organizations be wrong? In their book *Abolishing Performance Appraisals,* Tom Coens and Mary Jenkins point out that the research shows that performance evaluations do not work. "Our harsh censure of appraisal rests on a solid foundation. Academia, industry, and professional associations have intensely scrutinized appraisal for more than 50 years now, producing hundreds of studies, surveys, and articles. Despite a strong bias by many researchers who favor appraisal or imply that appraisal is indispensable, these studies and surveys offer scant evidence of appraisal's success."

Many companies, middle managers, indeed managers at all levels want to believe that their evaluation systems are worth the time and effort. Although it may make intuitive sense to review performance once or twice a year, the evidence that performance evaluations are not effective is clear. Why? For the simple reason that, in most companies, managers dread doing performance evaluations and employees dislike receiving them.

Moreover, many evaluations are not accurate. Few employees receive a truthful review, because their managers would rather deliver a positive evaluation. One reason for this is that managers do not want employees to think their performance is negative or lacking. This makes for an awkward and uncomfortable conversation that many managers prefer to avoid. Second, managers may grade an employee's performance higher than it actually is because they do not want to hurt their employee's chances of getting a raise or promotion.

Although there are significant differences in how performance evaluation systems may work, the results of studies are similar. Even companies that use detailed and structured evaluation systems have been largely unable to show a link between the evaluation process and performance improvement. Those who favor evaluation systems often cite the following reasons:

- The evaluation system documents performance and provides a paper trail in case of legal issues in the future (like a wrongful termination suit).
- The evaluation system identifies high and low performers. The evaluation process weeds out poor performers. Top performers get the recognition they deserve when they receive an outstanding evaluation.
- The evaluation process ensures that managers have formal performance conversations with their employees.
- The evaluation system promotes discussions that clarify the expectations managers have of their employees.

These beliefs may be true but, interestingly enough, do not directly foster improved performance—except in the case of the last point. While it is important for employees to be clear about expectations, relying on a performance evaluation session to accomplish this is not wise. Because both the manager and the employee want to get the evaluation conversation over with as soon possible, it is unlikely that any quality discussion is going to occur. Even top performers usually prefer to skip the formal evaluation discussion.

Why use unpopular, ill-designed, and fruitless performance evaluation systems? As well as being ineffective, evaluation systems take up substantial time and resources. Middle managers should not rely on a performance evaluation process to help improve individual or team performance. Techniques for improving performance are the focus of Chapter 11.

Myth #3: Employees prefer a sugarcoated counseling session to a candid one.

Middle managers who fail to get to the point and do not have the courage to speak plainly and candidly put their employees through an experience they should not have to endure. Employees know when their manager is dancing around a subject or putting a positive spin on an otherwise negative message. It is more effective (and humane) to communicate the concern in specifics and without any sugarcoating.

Many good managers falter when it comes to counseling their employees effectively. Managers will often sandwich criticism

CASE STUDY

Everyone agreed that Mindy was a great person and hard worker, but not a good manager of people. When Jim went to Mindy to discuss his concern that she was not ensuring her managers were working on the right tasks, Jim danced around the topic. He recognized that Mindy was busy and he said he knew she meant well and tried hard, and that her situation was unenviable. He expressed the concerns he had about her managers' productivity and why he felt this way. However, Jim did not clearly communicate the concerns that he had about Mindy's performance. Jim should have told her that her performance was not satisfactory, that she had not been managing her managers attentively, and that he expected her to fix the problem. When Jim left Mindy's office, she felt stressed, frustrated, and unsure of what Jim expected her to do. Throughout the conversation, Mindy could tell that Jim was dancing around the topic and wished he would get to the point and not make it drag on any longer than it had to.

between positive statements so the employee will not feel bad or react poorly. The sandwich technique doesn't work, however, because employees see right through the effort and don't focus on the important points conveyed. If a middle manager needs to counsel an employee, he or she should do so in a manner that is direct, clear, and candid.

Myth #4: Positive reinforcement is a great tool for improving performance.

Suzy had just received another "atta girl" from her manager for perfect attendance. Yesterday it was for getting the project done on time. Suzy's manager was always praising her for one thing or another. All this positive reinforcement should have made her feel great, but it didn't.

Many positive reinforcement practices backfire because they manage behavior, not optimize performance. Behavior modification, popularized by psychologist B. F. Skinner in the 1930s and 1940s, is a practice that works to shape and mold behavior. The basic idea is that when employees receive positive reinforcement, they are more likely to repeat the behaviors that elicited the praise. Conversely, negative reinforcement will cause an employee to do a particular behavior less often. Management-training programs that teach this technique often recommend delivering positive reinforcement five times more frequently than negative reinforcement. Some even ask managers to keep tick sheets to record the positive reinforcement they dole out.

Here's the problem: When positive reinforcement is part of a deliberate practice, it feels fake and manipulative. Employees can see through these techniques and end up feeling insulted rather than motivated. Managing by positive reinforcement is a practice that affects an employee's extrinsic motivation but rarely improves their intrinsic motivation. In fact, employees who work in an environment heavy in positive reinforcement will likely find work less intrinsically motivating. Tapping into an employee's intrinsic motivation is a better way to improve performance. (Strategies for improving intrinsic motivation appear in the next chapter.) For example, coming to work on time because you know you will be reprimanded if you do not is an example of being extrinsically motivated. You are motivated to do something because of what you will receive (positive or negative) as a result. Intrinsic motivation is a drive that comes from within and is based on a personally held value, belief, or goal. Extrinsic motivation is compliance based; intrinsic motivation is interest based. Positive reinforcement systems improve extrinsic motivation, but not intrinsic motivation. Managers who want to maximize performance will be more successful if they create an environment in which intrinsic motivation is improved, as this is where employee passion, drive, creativity, and energy come from.

It is important to distinguish positive reinforcement from appreciation. Employees do want to feel appreciated and that they make a difference. They want their managers to value and listen to them. Practicing positive reinforcement does not accomplish this.

Myth #5: Salary increases improve employee motivation and productivity.

At one company, salary increases occurred at the same time of the year for everyone. If salary increases improve employee motivation, one would have expected to see productivity go up after the raises took effect. Of course, this did not happen. In fact, there was no observable difference in performance or the employees' dispositions. Industrial psychologist Frederick Hertzberg studied the factors that bring about job satisfaction and dissatisfaction. He identified

> ### CASE STUDY
>
> Harry's team was in danger of losing several of its key members. Harry felt that to keep these talented managers, he would need to give them salary adjustments. However, what concerned the managers most was Harry's inconsistent and poor leadership. They wanted him to represent their needs to senior managers and thought he did not manage the department well. These managers were due for a raise and deserved one, but it was not the primary reason several were thinking of leaving the company. These managers were experiencing a great deal of daily hassle that was sapping them of much of their intrinsic motivation.

two groups of factors that affect employee satisfaction: hygiene factors and motivators. Hygiene factors include work conditions, pay, status, and security. When hygiene factors are poor, work is dissatisfying. When hygiene factors are acceptable, work is not dissatisfying. Adding more hygiene factors beyond what is satisfactory does not increase employee motivation. Hertzberg's motivators influence employee satisfaction based on fulfillment of higher-level, or intrinsic, needs. These needs include achievement, recognition, the quality of the work itself, and an opportunity for growth. Motivators improved worker satisfaction beyond where hygiene factors alone ever could.

Hertzberg's theory explained something that managers have seen in practice. Pay and other extrinsic rewards do not improve performance, nor do they increase an employee's overall motivation. When lacking or at a dissatisfactory level, these extrinsic factors can get in the way of employee motivation, but once satisfactory, have little impact on motivation or achievement.

The performance management practices described in the five myths damage individual and team performance. They stem from a command and control mindset about how to manage people. High impact middle managers know that tapping into their employees' hearts and minds is significantly more productive and fun. They know that employees want them to be great managers and communicate with them in a manner that is straightforward and authentic. Employees want to be appreciated and included in meaningful brainstorming and problem-solving conversations. High impact middle managers know that these things matter much more than gold stars, performance ratings, and other extrinsic rewards. The five myths about managing people illustrate what *not* to do to improve performance. Techniques for maximizing performance and satisfaction are offered in Chapter 11.

Chapter 11

Using H.I.M.M. Principles to Optimize Individual Performance

THE FIVE MYTHS ABOUT managing people presented in Chapter 10 described managerial practices that do not work. In addition to not being effective, these common practices are very labor and time intensive. There is a better way for middle managers to optimize individual performance! To encourage and facilitate great team member performance, middle managers need to understand and employ techniques based on beliefs about what it takes to influence peak performance in others. High impact middle managers spend their management time in productive ways that yield better results. They focus on the few performance-optimizing practices that offer the greatest benefit. And although middle managers are managers, the best do not manage people in the common sense of the word "management." They manage workflow, processes, systems, and communication. They enable their employees, but do not manage them. To optimize performance, your goals should be to:

- Get the work done well and on time.
- Ensure the right people are in the right jobs.
- Facilitate an environment where improvement and creativity happen.

Middle managers who select the right people, support them, and clearly communicate expectations will find that their employees, by and large, will manage themselves on a day-to-day basis. What employees need most is for their managers to clear the way so they can do their best work. To accomplish these objectives, middle managers should focus on the following five H.I.M.M. principles for optimizing individual performance:

1 ❯ Ensure that everyone knows what he or she is expected to achieve.
2 ❯ Have regular conversations, in clear and simple terms, about how each employee is or is not meeting expectations.
3 ❯ Do #1 and #2 in ways that maximize intrinsic motivation.
4 ❯ Take decisive and proactive action to deal with poor performers.
5 ❯ Be selective when hiring. Do not settle on someone who is not the right fit for the position or team.

H.I.M.M. Performance Principle #1: Ensure that everyone knows what he or she is expected to achieve.

As a middle manager, you can immediately improve the focus and productivity of your team members by ensuring that they know what is expected of them. When high impact middle managers talk to their employees, they go beyond discussing obvious expectations. They ensure that each person has a good understanding of how he or she can best contribute to the company. Notice the significant difference between the list of expectations discussed by most managers and those discussed by high impact middle managers.

The usual expectations conversation includes:
- Required tasks
- Project work
- Regular and ongoing work that the employee is responsible for
- The types of tasks that this person should own
- An expectation to bring questions and problems to the manager

The H.I.M.M. expectations conversation also includes:
- Expectations about how this person should contribute to identifying and solving problems
- Expectations about how this person will represent his or her function and the company
- Expectations about generating new ideas and improving results
- Expectations about how this employee should analyze and manage organizational resources (e.g., staff, finances, equipment)
- Expectations about how this person will manage employees
- Expectations about the business relationships this person should maintain and develop
- Expectations about deadlines, execution, and results
- Expectations about judgment and decisions
- Expectations about meeting preparedness and participation
- Expectations about planning and communicating work
- Expectations of how this person needs to improve his or her performance. For example, "Over the next year, I would like to see you more closely manage productivity in the A/P

area and improve speed and accuracy. This is an area where you have not been as attentive or effective."

The H.I.M.M. list of discussion topics may seem long, but it is necessary to ensure that each person fully understands what he or she is expected to accomplish. Middle managers who use the H.I.M.M. method of setting expectations will notice an immediate and welcome difference in their employees' focus because this approach fully communicates the breadth and importance of each person's role. Some employees may initially find this daunting or overwhelming; however, the ones who truly want to excel and do quality work will find this clarification of expectations motivating.

Do not get too prescriptive when discussing expectations. For example, it can be helpful to let the employee know how often he or she should provide progress updates. It is not helpful to define what the planning report should look like, how to disseminate work assignments, or the list of tasks included in the first report. That is micromanagement. Expectation conversations establish the measuring stick for performance, not the blueprint for how the employee is to conduct his or her work. If the employee could use a few tips on how to accomplish a task or project, schedule a separate coaching discussion to address this need.

A successful discussion will set up a powerful foundation for optimal performance and productivity. Clearly communicating expectations accomplishes more than any other performance-management activity and is at the top of the 80/20 list of great and right work to do.

Before the discussion:
- Think about and write down expectations. Type them up and make a copy to share with the employee.
- Talk to peers and other managers to ensure that assumptions about improvement areas are correct.

- Schedule the meeting at a time that is conducive to a relaxed and thorough discussion (not thirty minutes before a big meeting, or at 4:30 on Friday afternoon).
- Let the employee know that this discussion will focus on ensuring that he or she is clear about what is expected and how he or she can make a significant contribution to the company. Explain that clarifying expectations helps managers stay focused and successful. Other staff members will be scheduled for similar conversations.

During the discussion:
- This is no time to be wimpy or general—share expectations in clear, specific, and resolute terms. Cover all the areas, and more, on the H.I.M.M. list that are applicable to this person's job.
- Express expectations in a matter-of-fact manner. This is important to reduce the emotional content of the discussion. Expectation conversations should not become a sermon, plea, or sales pitch.
- Focus on the essential outcome—but allow some latitude on how to get there.
- Never assume that expectations are clear. Cover all expectations.
- Answer requests for clarification, but do not allow the meeting to creep into other topics. The desired outcome of this discussion is that expectations are clear and understood.

After the discussion:
- Once the initial discussion has taken place, expectations can be reinforced in a variety of day-to-day settings. Doing so will also help others in the organization understand each person's role and responsibilities.

- Be sure to follow up on expectations that are not being met. Do not wait to address concerns or issues, because doing so implies that it was not really an expectation.

Many employees do not fully understand what is expected of them, which is a shame because it impairs satisfaction, productivity, and results. By using H.I.M.M. techniques for clarifying expectations, you can ensure that your employees are focused on the right objectives and are set up for success.

> H.I.M.M. Performance Principle #2: Have regular conversations, in clear and simple terms, about how the employee is or is not meeting expectations.

Many middle managers are uncomfortable with and fear providing performance feedback. This discomfort becomes greater when they need to address inadequate performance. Managing performance is a fundamental responsibility for all middle managers and yet is the most dreaded and most often ignored. Talking to people about their performance can be awkward and scary, but there are rewards for getting past the discomfort. Productivity, efficiency, teamwork, employee satisfaction, and retention improve with effective performance management.

One of the primary reasons performance discussions are awkward is that they can be emotional. Don't try to make the message more palatable by stretching out the discussion or trying to be the employee's friend. Neither should you go to the other end of the toughness spectrum and come across as cold, hard-hitting, and critical. Either approach will likely provoke an emotional response from the employee who will hear the concerns as a personal assault and become defensive, angry, guilty, sad, or anxious.

Another reason managers hesitate to provide performance feedback is that they may feel uncomfortable being the leader. Talking with employees about what they are not doing well can make you feel like their parent or superior, which can be undesirable and unpleasant.

The H.I.M.M. process for discussing poor performance focuses on the exchange of simple, clear, and direct information that hopefully leads to a mutual understanding of the situation and what is needed in the future. This process limits emotional content and stresses improvement and success. This process minimizes the controlling or bosslike attributes of most feedback and emphasizes collaboration. The H.I.M.M. method is easier for the middle manager who has to deliver the message and more favorable for the employee who has to receive it.

High impact middle managers know how to discuss performance concerns in a matter-of-fact way that is quick, to the point, and clear. They talk to their employees about what is working and what isn't. While some performance concerns will warrant a dedicated meeting, daily discussions usually suffice for dealing with most concerns. The less it looks or feels like an event or scolding, the more effective the discussion. Here are a few examples of what H.I.M.M. performance conversations look like.

Scenario #1—As Part of Normal Day-to-Day Conversation

H.I.M.M.: Sue, let's chat about this morning's product-review meeting. The meeting went on a bit too long and got off track in a few places, don't you agree?

SUE: Yeah, I was trying to control it, but you know how some of those folks are. . . .

H.I.M.M.: Sure, there is always a good chance in a group that size that someone is going to get off topic. That's why I think it is important to have a detailed agenda, desired outcomes, and advanced notice of how each member should contribute to the meeting. We've talked about your role in leading effective meetings before and I know you know what to do. You probably just ran out of time or forgot to do all the prep.

SUE: Yes, a lack of time is part of the reason, but I also thought the meeting was going to be more simple and straightforward than it was.

H.I.M.M.: I can understand that, but meetings soak up a lot of time. Will you make sure to create and communicate an agenda for next week's meeting?

SUE: I will. I was planning on doing that for sure.

H.I.M.M.: Terrific. Now, do you have a few minutes to talk about the new product launch? I'd like to get your ideas about how we might find a few new vendors. . . .

Scenario #2—A Scheduled Performance Conversation

H.I.M.M.: Kay, I want to talk to you about the two-year vendor contracts. They were due two weeks ago, and I just learned that several are still outstanding. What is holding up the remaining contracts?

KAY: Well, as you know, I rely on the managers in each division to get their contracts in to me. I call them every few days, but some are just running behind.

H.I.M.M.: We need vendor contracts for our budgeting process. I would have expected you to bring this delay to my attention before the deadline. You are responsible for delivering on this timeline, and you need to do whatever it takes to get as many of these contracts in as possible. Had I known about the problem, I could have helped you find a solution. Now that the deadline has passed, let's talk about what you can do to get the outstanding contracts in as soon as possible. Would you like my help now in brainstorming ideas or would you prefer to think about it on your own and discuss it later this afternoon?

KAY: Let me think about it. I want to determine the issues affecting each contract first because there might be different options for how to ensure their completion.

H.I.M.M.: Great, my last meeting ends at three thirty; let's chat then. If you need someone to help you pull files, ask Denise. The project I have her working on is not as important as this. See you later.

The H.I.M.M. counseling conversation never communicates to the employee that he or she is bad, lacking, or a disappointment. These are devastating remarks to hear from a manager and would make it difficult for any employee to focus on solving the problem. Discussing the reason an employee is not performing as expected can leave him or her feeling bad and may get in the way of conversation about how to fix the problem. The H.I.M.M. method focuses on getting the employee into productive action and contains the following parts:

1 > Statement of the problem in factual terms (Here's what happened and why it is of concern . . .)
2 > Employee's acknowledgment of the problem
3 > A reaffirmation of the performance expected and a request to solve the problem
4 > A closing statement that shows there are no hard feelings, this is not personal, and that support and help are available if needed

Sue was a passionate and hardworking manager who got a bit emotional about her work. After the conversation with her manager in Scenario #1, it was clear that she needed to take a break before moving on to other topics of discussion. This was fine. Sue needed to think about the information and digest what she had heard. Middle managers need to be aware of what their employees need to be most productive. Different employees will have different needs. The H.I.M.M. techniques do not guarantee that the employee will not have an emotional reaction to the performance feedback, but they do lessen the possibility. In addition, employees will focus on fixing the problem and have a full understanding that it should not occur again.

The H.I.M.M. process for discussing outstanding performance also focuses on the simple, clear, and direct information. When an employee has done a great job, it is important to convey genuine appreciation in a way that does not look or feel like the positive reinforcement discussed in Chapter 10. In other words, express appreciation for work that makes a difference and is important. Here's how to express appreciation for a job well done:

- State specifically what the employee did well.
- Elaborate on the impact his or her work has on the team and company.
- Highlight the skills or behaviors used to do this work.
- Thank the person for making the team look good and for his or her hard work.
- Express personal gratitude.
- If possible or practical, ask him or her to share the achievement with others either by presenting his or her work in a meeting or by leading a related project.
- Ask managers (the next level of management or a peer middle manager whom this person's work affects) to express their gratitude as well.

H.I.M.M. Performance Principle #3: Do #1 and #2 in ways that maximize intrinsic motivation.

To move from mediocre to outstanding performance, employees need to have their hearts and minds fully engaged in the work they are doing. Intrinsically motivated employees produce this kind of productivity. That being the case, it is important that middle managers lead in ways that do not unintentionally wreck their employees' intrinsic motivation. This happens most often with middle managers who micromanage or rule with an iron fist. Employees of these managers feel manipulated and overmanaged, and this can kill any desire or passion they might have for the work.

Managers cannot control their employees' motivation, but they can establish a work environment that nurtures intrinsic motivation. Intrinsic motivation comes from within the person and refers to motivation to engage in an activity for its own sake. Intrinsically motivated people work on tasks because they find them enjoyable, satisfying, or meaningful. Intrinsic motivation is the inclination to seek out and master challenges; it is what motivates employees to do something they are not required to do.

Extrinsic motivation, on the other hand, is the drive to do a particular task as a means to an end. Extrinsically motivated employees put in effort to complete the work because they believe that doing so will result in a bonus, raise in pay, or other desirable outcome. Extrinsic motivation can also be a result of a compliance-driven workplace. Controlling factors such as rule books, bureaucracy, and narrow job roles are extrinsically motivating. The problem with extrinsic motivation is that it produces the minimum performance required to get a reward or avoid a negative outcome such as a reprimand or job termination. Extrinsically motivated employees do not have their heart and mind engaged in the work. It is common in business for managers to propose bonus structures and reward systems designed to improve performance, but this works only if performance is bad, and then it will raise performance to only a mediocre level.

High impact middle managers develop a work environment that allows intrinsic motivation to flourish. The elements that promote intrinsic motivation include:

1 > Work that is meaningful
2 > A feeling of progress, of making a difference
3 > Choice and discretion over one's day
4 > Work that exercises and engages the mind
5 > A feeling of ability and competence

H.I.M.M. techniques that stress these elements will naturally establish an intrinsically motivating workplace. You can take the following actions to optimize your employees' intrinsic motivation:

- Distribute the most interesting and challenging work among employees. Remember Jane? She kept the plum projects for herself and gave the average or boring assignments to her employees. This was a bad tactic because it excluded her employees from taking part in the most interesting work and did not build her organization's capacity.
- Encourage idea generation and unique approaches to problem solving. Allowing employees to play an active role in improving the business provides a sense that their work makes a difference.
- Encourage peers to help one another and share best practices.
- As much as it is practical, allow employees to define how to do their work. Giving them the latitude to decide how they will complete tasks improves the perception that they have choices and can exercise discretion.

- Know what each employee's interests and passions are and offer him or her projects and tasks that tap into those.
- Ensure that all employees grow and stay engaged in their work. Learning new skills and using them can be intrinsically motivating.
- Communicate the higher purpose and impact of the work they do.
- Allow employees to own whole tasks or projects instead of smaller parts.
- Empower employees to manage the piece of the business defined by their role. Resist the urge to step in and take over.
- Provide employees with the full information they need to be successful in their jobs. Communicate as much as is possible and appropriate.
- Celebrate achievements. Offer genuine acknowledgment to employees for outstanding work.
- Check out your own intrinsic motivation. Be an excellent role model and do whatever it takes to stay fully engaged in your work.

High impact middle managers who check the pulse of their work environment regularly will ensure that it is enriching and stimulating. This makes a significant positive difference in the overall performance and morale of the team. Tapping into employees' intrinsic motivations is the only way to enjoy peak performance levels.

H.I.M.M. Performance Principle #4: Take decisive and proactive action to deal with poor performers.

Jake was agonizing over what he had to do that morning. He was going to terminate one of his managers. Meg had worked for the company for three years. She was a hard worker but was a poor manager and poor strategist. Meg's employees disliked working for her because she was abrasive, manipulative, and played favorites. Jake had talked to Meg many times about her management style and her lack of strategic vision. Each time, she would put a good effort in for a few days but then slip back into her old ways. Meg's termination was well overdue, but that did not make it any easier for Jake. He preferred being the good guy, making people happy and handing out opportunities—not taking them away. After Meg left the building, it was as if a fog had lifted. Employees who were previously thinking about leaving the company felt a sense of hope. Not one person expressed regret that Meg had left the company. After seeing how the organization responded to Meg's departure, Jake kicked himself for waiting so long to take care of the problem.

Keeping a nonperformer is one of the most damaging decisions a middle manager can choose to make. Not only are the tasks of that individual's position not getting performed, but the productivity and morale of the entire organization are affected. Although it may be difficult to let an employee go, it is more difficult to see the team and individual flounder.

As a high impact middle manager, you should do everything you can to help each person succeed. However, when these efforts fail, and it is clear the fit is not right, you must take quick and decisive action to get the person out of the organization. Work with the HR department to make sure the proper documentation and cause exist, and then terminate the person. The best thing for all concerned is to get the termination over with quickly so everyone can move on.

Jim was in his office for a long time. He had begun the termination discussion with one of his employees over an hour ago, and there were no signs the conversation was ending. Jim was a deeply caring middle manager who did not know when to end a conversation! Many managers think it is humane to let the termination conversation drag out and get into a lot of detail, but that is usually a mistake. It is much more sensitive to keep the discussion short and focused. H.I.M.M. termination discussions get to the point quickly and efficiently.

- Let the person know that they are being terminated near the beginning of the conversation. Taking a lot of time to lead up to this point will only add to the stress, worry, and false hope of the employee. Letting the employee know he or she is terminated early in the conversation will speed up the time it is going to take them to process what is happening and be ready to discuss what is next.
- Speak in a tone that is matter-of-fact without being insensitive or uncaring. It is important to convey the decision without being emotional while communicating regret that the situation was not solvable.
- If the employee asks for another chance to improve his or her performance, hold firm by saying the decision is final and in the best interests of all involved to part ways.
- Move the discussion as quickly as possible to a review of the termination terms, severance, and what is going to happen when the employee leaves the meeting. Offer the option of clearing out his or her belongings after-hours to lessen his or her embarrassment and discomfort. Be as flexible with the terms and conditions as possible.
- Respect the person after he or she is gone by not badmouthing him or her in front of others and being respectful of what is said about his or her departure.

Most employees want to do a great job and can be significant team contributors. For the few employees who will not work out, speed of action and consummate professionalism will serve you and your department well in the long run.

H.I.M.M. Performance Principle #5: Be selective when hiring. Do not settle on someone who is not the right fit for the position.

One of the most effective ways to ensure that few termination conversations will have to take place is to hire the right people in the first place. Most terminations are the result of poor fit with the position. The desire to fill the position may tempt busy middle managers to accept a marginal candidate, but this is never the best solution. Hiring decisions are extremely important, and high impact middle managers keep their standards and expectations high. They know the best person is going to infuse the team with positive energy and valuable skills.

Peter Drucker, one of the world's most important management experts, said this about people decisions in his classic book *Management: Tasks, Responsibilities, Practices*: "The people decision signals to every manager of the organization what it is that management really wants, really values, really rewards. Placement and promotion are the most critical people decisions. They, above all, require careful thinking and clear policy and procedures, which live up to high standards of fairness and equity. They should never be made on the basis of opinions and on a man's 'potential.' They should always be based on the factual record of performance against explicit goals and objectives." Mr. Drucker stressed what most middle managers have seen in the workplace: that people decisions matter and communicate to the rest of the organization what it is looking for from its employees.

Middle managers who have outstanding team members will have a different management experience than that of their peers who are not so lucky. Everything is easier, better, more fun, and more effective when dealing with high-performing individuals. The H.I.M.M. techniques for hiring only the best include:

- Collaborate with HR to define and clarify desired skills and experience.
- Use specific behaviorally based questions that help discover what each candidate has done and how he or she approaches his or her work (the latter is often most important). If you are not skilled in interviewing techniques, then seek training or coaching, as this is necessary to make the right people decisions.
- Get to know the candidate's motivation for applying for this job. What does he or she want to get from the position? What work does he or she enjoy most? If a management position, make sure the candidate has a genuine interest in and capacity for management.
- Ask several people to interview each candidate. Ask each person to look for specific skills and qualities.
- When candidates are applying from within the organization, talk to managers and others who have worked with the person, and ask for their comments on whether that person would be a good fit for this role. Evaluate their results and ability to execute.
- Conduct thorough reference checks! Many managers think reference checks are a waste of time, but this is not the case if they are done well. Even discussions with references provided by the candidate (presumably their allies) can be illuminating. References will often help break a tie between two strong candidates or confirm a nagging feeling about the person's background.
- If there are no candidates who are a great fit, keep looking. Do not settle for a person who is available and convenient.

In the end, this will not benefit the organization or the person.

Middle managers who are picky about the people they bring onto their team will enjoy better results than their peers who are less selective. Each hiring decision communicates what you and the organization are looking for and the behaviors and skills that are most desirable. When the company hired Tim, an outstanding and energetic manager, the expectations for all managers got higher. By bringing Tim on, management had acknowledged that it valued proactive and creative managers and, in doing so, issued a subtle challenge to all other managers to show their best in these areas.

The H.I.M.M. principles for optimizing individual performance work because they focus on the few actions that will lead to the greatest results. These five practices reinforce one another because they share assumptions about performance. First, that most employees want to do a good job and make a positive difference. Second, that ensuring employees are clear about expectations prevents and resolves many performance problems. Third, that employees want to work for well-managed and productive teams.

High impact middle managers optimize performance by practicing the five H.I.M.M. performance principles consistently and methodically. They make sure team members are clear about what is expected of them and how well they are currently performing in regard to those expectations. The environment encourages and fosters intrinsic motivation through offering an inclusive and participative way for all team members to add value and make a difference. The team is comprised of highly talented folks who fit their roles and the team. High impact middle managers know that doing these things is the 20 percent that will yield 80 percent (or the greatest benefit) toward optimizing individual performance.

Chapter 12

H.I.M.M. Coaching — Helping Others Achieve Breakthroughs

ONE OF THE QUICKEST and most effective ways for a middle manager to impact his or her organization is through coaching. Coaching yields short-term and long-term payoffs. Helping others achieve breakthroughs boosts results today and builds the organization's skills for tomorrow. Unfortunately, coaching is an underutilized and poorly understood middle-management tool. Many managers confuse coaching with advice and counseling. **FIGURE 12.1** shows the similarities and differences among these three forms of influence. The areas where the circles intersect represent shared characteristics.

- The impetus for all three methods is to help the other person. Those who offer advice mean well, even though their opinions may be unwelcome.
- Both advice and counseling are directive and quick, but the receiver may welcome neither.
- Both advice and coaching address less urgent concerns and may consider the receiver's ideas.

- Both counseling and coaching focus on goals and may be effective for changing long-term behavior.
- Each method is useful in certain circumstances. Coaching is the only method of influence driven by the receiver, and it is the most valuable way to improve his or her effectiveness and success.

Coaching is different from advising, preaching, counseling, and persuading because the latter are all done from the viewpoint of and

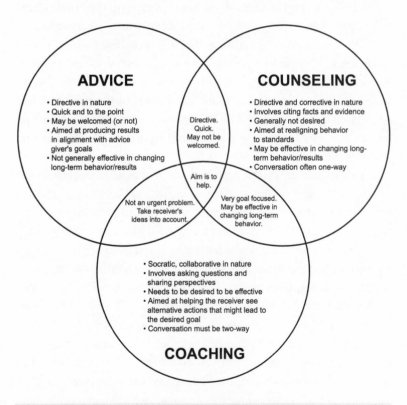

Fig. 12.1—Three ways to influence others

for the person offering it. Coaching is the exact opposite. A great coach talks little, listens a lot, and facilitates the thinking process of the receiver. When coaching, the focus is on goals and possibilities, not the receiver's performance.

Coaches offer their time to help the progress of another. Coaches never try to replace the receiver's goals with their own (this would become advice or counseling). Though coaching is altruistic in nature, it benefits the middle managers who employ it because it improves results. It is important to recognize both the altruistic and selfish aspects of coaching because doing so will help you choose coaching techniques that are most helpful to the receiver and the company.

Intrinsic motivation drives the best coaches to help others learn, grow, and perform. They get a charge out of helping people consider different viewpoints, and enjoy seeing the proverbial light-bulb turn on for people. Coaching can be one of the most fulfilling and meaningful roles a middle manager can play. By helping others move their work forward, you broaden your reach within and impact on the organization.

Being a coach is rewarding, but not always easy. Sometimes the coach needs to be willing to discuss undiscussables or help uncover unwritten rules getting in the receiver's way. Receivers may perceive things in a way that is detrimental to their success. Coaches help them clarify what's real and what's not. A coach needs to be tough to hold the receiver accountable for realizing his or her goals. Doing this in a way that does not come across as bossy or directive can be tricky, but great coaches know the secret lies in their intent to help, not control.

High impact middle managers have a genuine interest in knowing how to help employees and peers be successful. They have learned techniques for facilitating helpful conversations. High impact middle managers know that coaching must be voluntary and welcomed by the receiver, not forced. Forced coaching becomes advice or feedback. Receivers should do most of the talking during coaching conversations. Great coaches ask many questions but otherwise let the receiver talk about his or her goals, ideas, and setbacks. They know that it is through this dialogue the receiver is likely to see his or her challenge in a new and helpful way. Many people are comfortable with and welcome direction from their manager. Do not prescribe answers because this will prevent learning from taking place (you can, of course, help them learn where to go to get the answers!).

H.I.M.M. coaching helps middle managers and receivers get the most out of coaching discussions. The elements of H.I.M.M. coaching are as follows:

- Ad hoc coaching
- Formal coaching conversations
- Use of the Socratic questions
- Coaching infrastructures

Ad Hoc Coaching

Todd walked into Lou's office and asked for a few minutes to chat. Todd had an open position in his department, and he knew that it was going to be hard to fill. The tasks were so specific to the company that a current employee would be best to fill the job. Unfortunately, Todd could not think of a qualified internal candidate.

LOU: What skills and behaviors are you looking for?
TODD: This position requires analytical skills, knowledge of the business, a proactive leadership presence, and . . .
LOU: Do they really need to be strong in all of these areas? Do other members of the team have experience in these areas?

TODD: The other team members are strong, yes, and they have worked for the company for a long time. So the new person does not need to have it all.

LOU: Which skills are of highest importance? What about filling this position concerns you most?

TODD: Above all else, I need someone who is a self-starter and who will take charge of the function. What I fear most is not being able to drive improvements fast enough.

LOU: If this is the case, why does the person need to come from inside the company?

TODD: I guess they don't, but I would prefer it.

LOU: Okay, but keep challenging yourself on that assumption. Are there other positions that require similar skills and experiences?

TODD: There are a few I can think of . . .

LOU: Do any of the individuals in these positions have the behavioral qualities important for this job?

TODD: I am not sure.

LOU: Are there employees in the operations group who have these skills?

TODD: I don't know. I would not have thought of them. Perhaps there are.

LOU: Do you know of any managers whose strengths may not be a match to their current position?

TODD: Yes, there are a few people like that. . . . Hmmm. Wait a minute, I've got it. Thanks. I will talk to you later!

Ad hoc coaching can occur anytime and in various ways. A breakthrough can occur while chatting in the hallway. High impact middle managers seize opportunities to help their employees and peers. The dialogue between Todd and Lou is an example of ad hoc coaching. Middle managers practice ad hoc coaching when they take the initiative to ask questions that invigorate another person's thinking. Lou made it a habit to arrive a few minutes early to meetings. During this time, those around the table engage in small talk and share what is on the top of their mind. Lou had a knack for asking just the right question to help someone think about his or her problem in a new way. Lou would follow up with him or her after the meeting if it seemed like it would be helpful. Peers often shared their frustrations about projects they were struggling with and Lou would offer to help them brainstorm and organize their thoughts.

Many managers think they coach more than they actually do. In reality, though, giving advice is a far more common practice than coaching. The primary distinction between ad hoc coaching and advice is the number of open-ended questions that typifies coaching. In addition, a good coach will resist the urge to tell people what they should do. Techniques for providing excellent ad hoc coaching include:

- *Be available and accessible.* Ad hoc coaching can occur only if both parties have the time to talk. Middle managers who leave no time for informal discussions or who frequently close their office door will miss out on many opportunities to coach. Arrive at meetings a few minutes early, eat in the lunchroom, periodically have lunch with peers and employees, and stroll through the office several times a day.
- *Listen.* Employees and peers will share what is on their mind and highest on their list of challenges and concerns. Pick up on conversations in meetings and casual conversations.
- *Use Socratic questions to draw out new information and ideas* (see examples later in this chapter). Express genuine interest and curiosity.
- *Facilitate action plans.* Receivers may have a difficult time putting their ideas and thoughts into an organized action

plan. Coaches can help the receiver take action by making it easier for him or her to get started.

- *Encourage.* The receiver may be looking for someone to say, "Go for it!" Coaches encourage others to try new approaches and stretch boundaries.

Ad hoc coaching is a fantastic way for you to enable results. Coaches who keep their eyes open and reserve their opinions will find ample opportunities to provide coaching and make a difference.

Formal Coaching Conversations

Ad hoc coaching works for many people and situations, but not all. Sometimes the best approach is to set aside time to have a more formal coaching conversation. Formal coaching conversations are most suitable for enabling large projects or personal goals to get off the ground. The primary reason for scheduling a formal coaching session is to ensure enough time is set aside to have a fruitful discussion. The coaching conversation will be more effective when the coach and receiver embrace the following roles:

The Coach's Role
- Asks the receiver to define his or her goal. What is he or she hoping to make happen?
- Keeps the discussion on track and moving.
- Asks questions that stimulate discussion (see the section on Socratic questions later in this chapter).
- Summarizes and clarifies discussion topics.
- Clarifies understanding of the receiver's goals and his or her motives for having those goals.
- Helps the receiver develop an action plan.

- Facilitates small victories for the receiver. For example, Lou knew that Denny wanted to learn more about other parts of the company and arranged for him to participate on a cross-functional project team. This assignment exposed him to several other functional groups and benefited the overall organization.

The Receiver's Role

The coaching conversation progresses as the coach asks questions and makes statements that help to further the receiver's thinking. The goal for this discussion is for the receiver to expand his or her viewpoint, generate new approaches to meeting his or her goals, and to dispel assumptions or beliefs that are getting in the way of progress. The receiver may change his or her goals based on new insights or information. When done well, the receiver leaves the coaching session energized with new ideas and a clearer focus.

- Shares his or her goal, desired outcome, ideas, and motivations for the goal.
- Discusses questions, frustrations, and problems he or she has already faced.
- Shares the information he or she has collected this far.
- Defines his or her basic interpretations, judgments, assumptions, and points of view.
- Reviews current progress he or she is making toward the goal and defines the barriers that are getting in the way.
- Is open to exploring new ideas and approaches.

Use of Socratic Questions

Middle managers who use Socratic questions collect useful information that helps them coach and lead their functions. As coaches, middle managers can help their employees and peers develop critical thinking and creativity skills. Socratic questions enable coaches to facilitate conversations in a more effective way.

The Socratic method, named for the Greek philosopher Socrates, emphasizes the use of thought-provoking questions to promote learning (instead of offering opinions and advice) and challenge widely held beliefs.

Socratic questions are those that are probing and open-ended. You can use these questions in a business context to help develop others. The inquiry process is the cornerstone of this practice because it helps receivers think creatively and solve problems using new approaches. Socratic questions also help the receiver clarify what he or she understands and what is yet unknown. Through this inquiry, strategies for improving effectiveness emerge while energizing the receiver's curiosity. Middle managers who use Socratic questions challenge the receiver in a way that is intrinsically motivating.

Below are examples of Socratic questions.

Questions That Clarify the Receiver's Goals
- What would you like to have happen?
- How would you like to see this happen?
- Why are you favoring a change?
- If everything goes well, what will it look like in __ mos./yrs.?
- In your mind, what will happen if we do not change?

Questions That Clarify the Receiver's Intent or Motives
- Why do you want this?
- Why do you say that?
- How would you benefit?
- Why is this important?
- What made you think of this?
- Who benefits from this?

Questions to Ensure the Receiver's Goals Are Aligned to Get Results

- How does this relate to your goal or objective?
- Where do you think this goal will lead?
- What does this mean?
- What do we already know about . . . ?
- Why is this your goal?
- What do you think will happen?

Questions to Uncover the Receiver's Basic Assumptions

- What basic assumptions do you have about this?
- Are there other assumptions that could also be valid?
- How do you know that what you believe is true?
- Do you agree with the following assumption: _____? Why/why not?
- What does _____ think about this situation?
- What would happen if . . . ?
- What are the consequences of that assumption?
- Why do you think I asked this question?
- What is it about the question that is difficult to answer?

Questions to Discover If the Receiver Has Enough Information

- What do you need to know about this?
- What generalizations can you make?
- What data have you looked at already?
- How do you know that _____?
- Why do you think this is occurring?
- How can you be sure?
- Have you seen a situation like this before?
- What do you think is the cause?
- What evidence is there to support your assertion?

Questions to Facilitate Seeing Other Points of View
- What would be an alternative?
- Is there another way to look at it? Why is it better?
- What are the pros and cons of this approach?
- How is this similar or different from what you have done in the past?
- What is the counterargument?
- What would someone who is against this idea say?
- What other ideas have you explored?
- How does this affect _____?

Socratic questions improve the coach's ability to remain objective by directing responses and conclusions back to the receiver. They also ask the receiver to consider many facets of a problem or goal, increasing the chances that new learning will occur.

Coaching Infrastructures

As a middle manager, you should think about how coaching can best be delivered in your organization. Some companies, like Bell Atlantic and Intel, have utilized formalized coaching structures. Coaches are trained, assigned, and expected to meet at regular and ad hoc times. Often, these coaching structures also document goals and one's progress in reaching them. Intel's mentoring program uses their company intranet to match partners (the learner) with potential mentors. Mentors and partners work toward goals stated in their mentoring contract. Meeting frequency and design are left up to the mentor and partner.

Former CEO Raymond Smith described coaching at Bell Atlantic (now Verizon) as an important part of their management culture. "Coaching is not seen as the least bit corny or unusual in our company. Once a week, one of us will ask, 'Can I coach you on something?' In the past, I have never been able to do that comfortably. I was never able to do it without it being unnecessarily evasive on the one hand or unpleasant on the other. Now the process is acceptable. It is group sanctioned. It's the way we've decided we're going to work together."

The pros of a formalized coaching structure include:
- Coaching becomes part of the culture of the business.
- Assignment of coaches removes the stigma and embarrassment some may associate with coaching.
- More people give and receive coaching under a formalized system.

The cons of a formalized coaching structure include:
- Under a formalized coaching structure, the chances increase that people participate because it is compulsory or a corporate sacred cow. Mandatory systems often diminish some of the intrinsic motivation that can be associated with coaching.
- Formalized systems can be resource intensive and costly.
- Many formalized systems may not be flexible enough to meet the different needs of a diverse management group. It's hard to please all the people all of the time.

Many companies, like Mead Paper and Amazon.com, do not utilize formalized coaching structures. In these types of organizations, coaching is encouraged and supported, but no formal training or expectations exist. (Companies often say that managers should coach their employees, but most are not really talking about coaching as it has been defined here.) Most companies fall into this category. At Amazon.com, dynamic, small team groups are utilized to encourage learning and development. Their formula is to hire diverse and smart people and let coaching and knowledge transfer happen by osmosis. This model can work if the environment is set up to encourage team problem solving and idea generation.

The pros of an informal coaching structure include:
- Coaching tends to be timely and need based.
- Those who are excellent coaches likely coach more than those who are poor coaches. In other words, the spontaneous and personal nature of the system will lead to certain people being sought out to coach more than others do. A natural selection, of sorts, for coaching.
- Coaching and being coached is likely to be more intrinsically motivating when it is not compulsory.

The cons of an informal coaching structure:
- Fewer people receive coaching and often the people who need it most do not seek out coaching.
- Coaches are less likely to receive valuable training.
- Without a structure to establish coaching as an important management tool, it is less likely to be valued and a high priority.

In addition to formal and informal coaching structures, there are coaching models that fit along the spectrum between these two. There is no right or wrong method or approach to how coaching will be offered in an organization. As a middle manager, you are in the best position to assess and understand the best way to utilize coaching to develop people. Work with your peers, manager, and training department to ensure that the appropriate coaching model is evaluated and implemented. Why go to these lengths? Coaching, done well, is one of the most powerful management tools you have.

High impact middle managers have learned that coaching and being coached are high-value-added activities that enable results.

H.I.M.M. coaching maximizes the impact you can have by employing various coaching techniques in many settings and contexts. As a middle manager, you can help your staff achieve breakthroughs by recognizing and utilizing daily coaching opportunities. Just remember that to be a great coach, it is first important to recognize what coaching is and is not. Giving someone your advice is not coaching. Whether you coach in an ad hoc or formal conversation, or as part of an established coaching structure, it is paramount that the coaching conversations be focused on and driven by the learner. By using the elements of H.I.M.M. coaching, you will find your ability to coach peers and employees improves. Performance management and problem-solving skills also benefit from a regular use of Socratic questions and other H.I.M.M. coaching techniques. By employing coaching in your daily management practice, you can build organizational capacity, heighten individual satisfaction, and intrinsically motivate others.

Part Five

Honing Your Craft as a H.I.M.M. Leader

Chapter 13

H.I.M.M. Coachability—How to Reach Goals Faster and Better

HIGH IMPACT MIDDLE MANAGERS need to be highly coachable. What does being coachable mean? Much of a middle manager's day is concerned with guiding others, coaching team members, and assisting peers. However, it is just as important that middle managers ensure that they are getting the coaching, input, and development they need to be successful and continue to grow in their position. Coachability, then, is the degree that you are open to what your environment can offer, or the extent to which you will accept and consider input and ideas.

High impact middle managers know that their success depends on their being highly coachable when it counts most. Although all managers will be coachable some of the time and uncoachable during other moments, the most effective middle managers will be more coachable overall and, most importantly, during the times when it can make the greatest difference.

What Coachability Looks Like

Coachability is measured by how well a manager interacts with his or her environment; therefore, it is visible and observable behavior. Coachability is easy to recognize in others. When a manager is being coachable, there is an open, curious, and relaxed quality to his or her demeanor. When highly coachable, he or she:

- Is not defensive when challenged or offered an alternative view
- Welcomes feedback and ideas for improvement
- Asks for coaching
- Considers and uses ideas offered by others
- Seeks training and development in the form of reading, classes, new assignments, and coaching from others
- Has a good sense of his or her strengths and weaknesses
- Handles failures and setbacks with grace

Being coachable usually goes hand in hand with confidence and a positive impression of one's own skills and abilities. Coachable managers display a sense of calm and a focus that allow them to take ideas and process them without feeling the need to defend or rationalize current methods. Highly coachable managers genuinely welcome and accept alternative points of view.

Middle managers who are being uncoachable are also easy to identify. They put up barriers between themselves and others. Uncoachability often looks like this:

- They do not listen to ideas offered by others.
- They staunchly defend current ideas and approaches.
- They believe they must do things on their own and that asking for input is a sign of weakness.
- They appear to be nonreceptive or not interested in coaching.

- They do not engage in conversations about development with their manager, and view suggestions that they should develop new skills as criticism.
- They can be dismissive of others.

By observing how your peers behave during meetings and work sessions, you can begin to notice the behavioral cues that signal whether they are coachable or not. You should also seek to recognize these behaviors in yourself! Recognizing when you are being uncoachable is an important step toward improving your ability to accept constructive criticism.

Coachability Is a State of Mind

It is important to emphasize that people are not inherently coachable or uncoachable. Everyone has moments during which they are coachable and others during which they are not. Saying that someone is not a coachable person unfairly classifies him or her and does not recognize that coachability is a way of being that can be chosen in any given moment.

Middle managers interested in increasing their coachability need to examine what triggers their uncoachable moments. By understanding your personal triggers, you can recognize them and choose to be more coachable when the opportunity presents itself in the future. Here are some examples of various emotional triggers:

- People triggered Harry's uncoachability when they questioned his decisions or opinions in front of his managers. He had a strong need to be right, and when challenged, he became uncoachable.

- Kathy refused to hear feedback if the suggested idea changed or altered her tidy existence. She took great pride in planning her work, and when an idea had the potential to turn her world upside down, she resisted it regardless of its merit or potential.
- Jim was often uncoachable when overwhelmed with too many tasks to do. His peers and managers eventually learned that it was best to save ideas or suggestions for another day if Jim had a backlog of projects or meetings.
- Corky was coachable when talking with others in her field of expertise but quickly became defensive with suggestions offered from individuals outside her department.

All middle managers encounter circumstances or people who trigger their uncoachability. Understanding and recognizing the obstacles that get in the way of your coachability is the first step toward becoming more receptive and, therefore, more successful. For example, a trigger for uncoachability may be something as simple as the time of day. You may find that you, or a peer, are not receptive to coaching at the end of a busy day that has been filled with meetings and projects. If you are sensitive about getting feedback or constructive criticism, you may prefer to schedule coaching sessions earlier in the morning, before the majority of staff arrives or after most people have left the office and you are free of distractions. The size and composition of the group might also make a difference in how open you are to coaching. Do you prefer coaching sessions to be one-on-one or with immediate peers? Are you less receptive to coaching if senior managers are present?

Even high impact middle managers are human. It is important for you to be aware of your mood and recognize when you are not feeling coachable. It is better to reschedule a conversation or meeting for another time than be uncoachable and get little from the conversation. Once you become aware of what your triggers or resistance points are, you can open yourself up to more opportunities for improvement and perhaps a breakthrough.

Coachability as a Definition of Success

High impact middle managers strive to be extremely teachable. They adopt the belief that being highly coachable is important if they are to be successful. Coachable managers have altered their definition of what respect and competence look like. They know that they will be well regarded and held in higher esteem if they openly accept ideas and suggestions from others.

How Dell Encourages Coachability

⟫ Given that survival in the high-tech field is incumbent on staying ahead of the knowledge curve, Michael Dell, CEO of Dell Computer Corporation, cites coachability as a key requirement for himself as well as the managers in his company. In his bestselling book *Direct from Dell: Strategies That Revolutionized an Industry,* Dell had this to say about learning: "Our people are obviously motivated by the ways we link our goals to their compensation and incentives. But more importantly, there are ways in which we work to instill ownership thinking in our people and better leverage their talents so they can reach their full potential. The willingness and ability to learn constantly is one of them. . . . I approach learning from the standpoint of asking questions: What would make your job at Dell easier? What do our customers like and not like? What would they like to see us doing better? How can we improve? I start by asking a lot of questions and doing a lot of listening: You don't learn anything when you're talking."

Stimulating, open, and meaningful conversations encourage coachability and learning. Middle managers who employ Dell's method of asking numerous open-ended questions will find that the coachability of others improves. The discussions that come out of such a dialogue will yield creative and useful ideas.

High impact middle managers know they will be much more successful if they focus on getting the best results, which comes from hearing and using the advice of many, rather than on being right. They regularly ask for input and coaching from many different people.

Techniques for Improving Your Coachability

In addition to recognizing when you are being coachable or uncoachable and embracing the belief that being coachable is important for success, there are several specific techniques you can use to improve your coachability. These methods will also help high impact middle managers improve their ability to solve problems and generate creative opportunities.

- Coachability starts with a mindset. When you notice that you are being uncoachable, pause, take a deep breath, and decide to let go of the feelings of resistance and be more open.
- Ask more open-ended questions to glean more information about projects and processes.
- Ask follow-up questions to understand ideas and suggestions fully.
- Take the initiative to ask for input on one problem, idea, or topic each day.
- Resist the urge to defend yourself or say why an idea won't work. Focus on the desired outcome, not on being right.
- Schedule brainstorming and problem-solving meetings during the time of day or week that you are most coachable.

These techniques can help you immediately improve your overall coachability and ensure that you are being coachable when it matters most. High impact middle managers have developed the ability to monitor their coachability and quickly choose behaviors that support that. They have learned that becoming more coachable is a test of mind over matter that gets easier with practice and experience.

Using Coachability to Attract a Breakthrough

Breakthroughs happen when people let them. Sometimes middle managers are like sponges, happily soaking in new information. All too often, however, preconceived notions, fears, and the ego shut out the opportunities that these managers seek. Coachability is the level of openness a manager has to outside influences and development. There is a strong positive relationship between breakthroughs and high coachability. Middle managers who want to experience breakthrough results can improve their odds by careful preparation of their work environment and themselves. To attract a breakthrough, try these ten methods:

1 > Let peers, managers, and employees know the topics or challenges of greatest interest and importance. The more people enrolled in a challenge, the better the chances that a terrific idea or approach will surface.

2 > Call a meeting to brainstorm ideas and suggestions. Encourage diverse points of view and a variety of ideas. Go beyond inviting the most logical people to the meeting and include those who have had great ideas about other problems.

3 > Seek nontraditional avenues of information and ideas. Read current research and periodicals related to this topic.

4 > Don't be shy. Call or e-mail top thinkers and researchers in the field and ask for their perspectives.

5 > Focus on defining the ideal desired outcome and asking questions about what conditions would need to exist to support this outcome.

6 > Take, and be fully engaged in, a class on the subject.

7 > Make a request you would normally consider unreasonable. It generally does not hurt to ask and may even work! Most middle managers are so conservative about what they ask for that their unreasonable requests are not likely to be that unreasonable.

8 > Adopt a "this shall be" mindset. There seems to be some legitimacy to the self-fulfilling prophecy (when an expectation appears to lead to or cause the anticipated outcome), so managers might as well have this phenomenon work in their favor.

9 > If important enough, ask an outside facilitator to lead a group of people through a work session to brainstorm ideas, approaches, barriers, and desired outcomes. Professional facilitators can often detect the dynamics of the group and guide the discussion for the best outcome.

10 > Benchmark other admired and respected companies who do this particular task or process extremely well.

Breakthroughs are improvements that lead to a significant change. This change can be physically tangible, such as a new process or product, or in your mind, such as a new way of looking at an old problem. Either way, you can increase your odds of experiencing a breakthrough by taking the initiative to establish an environment that will support breakthrough thinking.

Coachability Opens Doors

Middle managers who increase their number of coachable moments will find the door of opportunity opens wide. Possibilities never thought possible become real and obstacles fall by the wayside. Highly coachable middle managers are also highly promotable! Senior managers respect and value managers who do whatever it takes to produce the best results. Coachable managers will get more done and will utilize and implement more creative solutions than their peers who are less coachable.

Some middle managers do not value coachability because they believe they need to appear strong and confident. Do not confuse confidence with ego. High impact middle managers are strong, confident leaders *and* they are highly coachable. When middle managers can demonstrate confidence and coachability, they improve their ability to get results through people and enjoy a successful career with many new and interesting challenges.

Coachability is an important qualification for high impact middle managers. Middle managers need to be coachable to meet the diverse and challenging requirements of their jobs. By recognizing what coachability looks like and by employing techniques that enhance coachability, you can improve your results and effectiveness. Being coachable is a very engaged and interested state of mind—a feeling many find intrinsically motivating. Moving fast in the right direction feels great. Increased success and respect are great tonics that will reinforce the benefits of being coachable.

Chapter 14

The H.I.M.M. System—Putting It All Together for Maximum Managerial Flow

As was described in the introduction to this book, high impact middle management has a rhythm, or a flow, that can be intensely satisfying and successful. In his book *Beyond Boredom and Anxiety,* Mihaly Csikszentmihalyi described the flow experience as one where moments flow in a unified, focused, and intrinsically stimulating manner. High impact middle managers often experience flow at work. They are talented, prepared, and energized to make things happen. They have internalized their role and the beliefs that will serve them best. These managers have tried and now habitually practice most of the techniques presented in this book.

Reread the first two paragraphs of the introduction. Have you ever had a day like that? If you have, you undoubtedly know that it is something that you don't think about as it is occurring—it just happens. When at the top of your game, you are not likely to think about what you are doing or how you are doing it. Middle managers who internalize the H.I.M.M. system in their own way and style will enjoy the flow experience more often than their peers who do not. Why? H.I.M.M. is designed with several important elements of flow in mind, including fun, challenge, excitement, contribution, and focus. Sound familiar? These are also common intrinsic motivators.

To pull the H.I.M.M. system together for maximum managerial flow, you will want to ensure that you love your job and are feeling a sense of accomplishment and satisfaction that comes with having impact and making a difference. You will want to have fun with your work! So please use the techniques offered as part of the H.I.M.M. system, but do so in the way that works best for you.

You likely have noticed that there are two types of suggestions offered by H.I.M.M. First and foremost, there are beliefs, mindsets, and ways of thinking. Second, the system offers pragmatic tools and practices suggested by the H.I.M.M. belief set, or definition of success. To begin internalizing the H.I.M.M. system, take on some of the beliefs and try them. Often, the techniques will easily follow from that.

Where should you begin? The most important suggestion for how to get started is to get started! Getting into action and trying the H.I.M.M. system is more important than how you do it or with which technique you begin. Because the system elements support and reinforce one another, it does not matter where you start. Just start.

Keeping the H.I.M.M. System Top of Mind—The Scorecard

Regularly reviewing the beliefs and practices will help you internalize the H.I.M.M. system. As presented in Chapters 2 and 5, clarifying goals and communicating them to others improves performance. Middle managers who clarify their personal management development goals and refer to them often will outperform managers who set and then forget about goals. The H.I.M.M. Scorecard is a synopsis of the system's elements and techniques. An 8 x 11-inch version of the H.I.M.M. Scorecard is available for download at *www.haneberg-management.com.*

How to use the H.I.M.M. Scorecard

Middle managers can begin to put the H.I.M.M. system methods and tools to work for them by reviewing the scorecard at the beginning of each day. In time, application of the summarized gems found on the scorecard will become second nature. This will enable the middle manager to access the tools more readily, recognize opportunities to put H.I.M.M. to work for him or her, and encourage the flow experience.

Using the ROR Cheat Sheet as a tool for breakthroughs

On the back of the H.I.M.M. Scorecard is a reprint of the RORs, as presented in Chapter 1. This ROR Cheat Sheet can help middle managers diagnose potential response problems and opportunities for specific problem areas such as a project that has stalled or a problem that won't go away.

The ROR Cheat Sheet works by prompting you to think about how you have been approaching a particular problem and will offer potential alternative approaches. Teams can use the ROR Cheat Sheet to help them solve problems and implement improvements. The cheat sheet is also a good reference for staff or planning meetings.

Conclusion: It Is Just the Beginning!

Honing one's craft is a satisfying and fruitful endeavor. It takes time, commitment, and a passion for the work. Each new idea, skill, method, experience, and tool adds to the high impact middle manager's knowledge bank and allows him or her to develop his or her own brand of management. Middle-management growth and development is a rich and tailored process that provides organizations with the diverse and creative talent needed to prosper. The objective of the H.I.M.M. system is to add to your cache of methods for dealing with complexity, setbacks, and possibilities. Each middle manager will interpret and take different things from H.I.M.M.

Some may strive for sameness, but differences are what energize the field of management. Whereas diversity of thought, action, and approach benefits organizations, there are basic propositions that underlie the individual approaches of the most successful middle managers, those referred to here as high impact middle managers. These propositions are presented and reinforced throughout this book. Therefore, while you should follow your individual path for using H.I.M.M. techniques, keep the following things in mind.

- High impact middle managers are driven to make things better. They know their roles exist to move work forward in ways that would not occur without them.
- Successful middle managers are proactive. There is simply too much going on every day, and reactive managers cannot accomplish the needed work.
- High impact middle managers know they are important and make a difference. They take their roles seriously and possess professionalism commensurate with it. They know they are role models and the perpetuators of corporate culture.
- High impact middle managers believe that the most important work they do is management. They measure accomplishment in terms of management successes in addition to numbers of widgets produced.
- Managers don't control people, and control-oriented performance-management approaches can never maximize individual

performance. High impact middle managers have learned to temper their need to control people and instead focus on controlling their own behaviors, as well as departmental processes and systems.

■ Employees, peers, and managers want their middle managers to be at their best and to continue to develop new skills. Conventional thinking might lead managers to believe that, as they move up the corporate food chain, they have less to learn and do not need as much coaching. High impact middle managers have figured out that this is not the case. To provide the value and contribution the organization and team members seek, middle managers need to learn more and receive more coaching than frontline supervisors do. The middle manager's job is different, and the scope of responsibility immense.

■ High impact middle managers know that one of the most important choices they make each day is how to spend their limited time.

These themes are common among the best middle managers and run through the H.I.M.M. system. They are imbedded in the guiding principles and can be found as elements to the dozens of techniques and tools offered here. High impact middle managers have figured out what they need to do to maximize short-term and long-term results, and they do those things. Their work is successful and fruitful. High impact middle managers cover a lot of ground in their organizations. Therefore, the middle manager's breadth of responsibility is significant and the best have learned how to impact results across the organization. Senior executives expect their middle managers to influence every level of the company, and H.I.M.M. helps middle managers effectively reach the people and processes that need their attention and guidance.

This book seeks to reveal the compelling and intriguing elements of the middle manager's job so that current middle managers appreciate the work they do and those not currently in the field will want in. Professionals interested in making a significant contribution to their organization and gaining great satisfaction from their work know that being a middle manager can provide these rewards.

Please use this book often and as a reference. Good luck as you hone your middle-management craft. Enjoy the path and the destination, as the ride can be just as invigorating as the finish. Here's to experiencing the magic and flow of High Impact Middle Management!

Appendix

Additional H.I.M.M. System Information Available

The following resources can be found at *www.haneberg-management.com*.

The H.I.M.M. Scorecard (Chapter 14) and ROR Cheat Sheet (Chapter 1)
The H.I.M.M. Scorecard contains many of the key points made in this book. It is an at-a-glance version of the H.I.M.M. system.

The H.I.M.M. Definition of Success Cheat Sheet
The H.I.M.M. Definition of Success Cheat Sheet summarizes several powerful middle-management beliefs. Middle managers who choose to take on these beliefs will improve their effectiveness and may produce a breakthrough. This cheat sheet allows middle managers to modify or add to the listed beliefs to create a customized definition of success.

The H.I.M.M. Playbook (Chapter 5)
The H.I.M.M. Playbook is a planning and communication tool for middle managers that combines goal setting, work planning, and prioritization. The playbook gets its inspiration from sports playbooks.

The H.I.M.M. Reputation Survey (Chapter 4)
The H.I.M.M. Reputation Survey is a tool middle managers can use to learn more about the reputation they have built in their organization.

List of Recommended Reading for Middle Managers

Abolishing Performance Appraisals: Why They Backfire and What to Do Instead by Tom Coens and Mary Jenkins (Berrett Koehler)
Beyond Boredom and Anxiety by Mihaly Csikszentmihalyi (Jossey-Bass)
Circle of Innovation by Tom Peters (Alfred A. Knopf)
Control Your Destiny or Someone Else Will: Lessons in Mastering Change by Noel M. Tichy and Stratford Sherman (HarperInformation)
Direct from Dell: Strategies That Revolutionized an Industry by Michael Dell with Catherine Fredman (HarperBusiness)

The Empowered Manager: Positive Political Skills at Work by Peter Block (Jossey-Bass)

The Essential Drucker: The Best of Sixty Years of Peter Drucker's Essential Writings on Management by Peter Drucker (HarperBusiness)

Execution: The Discipline of Getting Things Done by Larry Bossidy, Ram Charan, and Charles Burck (Contributor) (Crown Publishing Group)

The Fifth Discipline by Peter Senge (Currency)

Flight of the Buffalo: Soaring to Excellence, Learning to Let Employees Lead by Ralph Stayer and James Belasco (Warner Books)

The Goal: A Process of Ongoing Improvement by Eliyahu M. Goldratt and Jeff Cox (North River Press)

Good to Great: Why Some Companies Make the Leap . . . and Others Don't by Jim Collins (HarperCollins)

How to Win Friends & Influence People by Dale Carnegie, Dorothy Carnegie, and Arthur R. Pell (Pocket Books)

Management: Tasks, Responsibilities, Practices by Peter Drucker (Harper & Row)

Managing Transitions: Making the Most of Changes by William Bridges (Addison-Wesley)

Masterful Coaching: Extraordinary Results by Impacting People and the Way They Think and Work Together by Robert Hargrove (Jossey-Bass)

Maverick: The Success Story Behind the World's Most Unusual Workplace by Ricardo Semler (Warner Books)

Out of the Crisis by W. Edwards Deming (MIT Press)

Punished by Rewards: The Trouble with Gold Stars, Incentive Plans, A's, Praise, and Other Bribes by Alfie Kohn (Houghton Mifflin)

Reengineering the Corporation: A Manifesto for Business Revolution by Michael Hammer & James Champy (HarperBusiness)

Seven Habits of Highly Effective People by Stephen R. Covey (Simon & Schuster)

The Social Construction of Reality: A Treatise in the Sociology of Knowledge by Peter L. Berger and Thomas Luckman (Anchor Books)

Stewardship: Choosing Service or Self-Interest by Peter Block (Berrett Kohler)

Thriving on Chaos: Handbook for a Management Revolution by Tom Peters (Harper & Row)

What the CEO Wants You to Know: How Your Company Really Works by Ram Charan (Crown Publishing Group)

Web Site Resources for Middle Managers

www.haneberg-management.com—Web site dedicated to the practice and science of management.

www.hbr.com—*Harvard Business Review* online. Download and purchase articles on almost any management and leadership topic.

www.fortune.com—Online home of *Fortune* magazine. Always interesting and allows for searching of old articles.

www.fastcompany.com—Web site for *Fast Company* magazine, which is one of the more creative and innovative business magazines available to middle managers.

www.1800ceoread.com—CEO Read (formerly Schwartz Business Books) is a terrific place to find information about business books.

www.tompeters.com—Tom Peters's Web site always has lots of interesting information. Tom is still thought-provoking after all these years!

www.pfdf.org—The Leader to Leader Institute (formerly the Peter F. Drucker Foundation for Nonprofit Management).

www.businessweek.com—*BusinessWeek* magazine online.

online.wsj.com—*The Wall Street Journal* online.

Want to Learn about High Impact Middle Management at Work?

Thanks for purchasing and reading this book. Middle managers can learn more about how to become a high impact middle manager at their workplace. Contact company training professionals or the HR department and ask them to inquire about the options listed below.

The H.I.M.M. trainer's guide

Middle managers can learn the H.I.M.M. system at their workplace. Companies with management-development professionals are able to receive middle-management training using *H.I.M.M.: Solutions for Today's Busy Managers* as the text. A facilitator's manual is available for training professionals who would like to conduct training sessions for their middle managers. There are several advantages of providing the H.I.M.M. system training in-house:

1 **❯** Facilitated workshops will product better results than reading alone can. Middle managers will learn and be able to apply the H.I.M.M.

skills more fully and effectively as a result of attending the training work-shops. The facilitated workshops offer more examples and exercises that help illustrate the techniques and tools. The workshops are designed to promote group discussion and exploration of H.I.M.M. system elements.

2 > Middle managers will benefit from learning the H.I.M.M. system as a group. When peers learn the same methods together, they are able to utilize each other as coaches and supporters. The H.I.M.M. techniques will quickly become part of the language middle managers use at work. This collective practice will reinforce the H.I.M.M. methods and processes. H.I.M.M. facilitators will also become resources for middle managers.

3 > Learning the H.I.M.M. system is easier when facilitated over sev-eral workshop sessions. Each session has a different focus, which builds on previous topics. Additional examples and exercises give middle managers more ideas for how to improve their results using H.I.M.M.

4 > The process of attending middle-management training with peers will produce a side benefit of building stronger peer relationships and partnerships, and the H.I.M.M. system workshops are designed to be fun, mentally stimulating, and engaging.

Training professionals interested in facilitating H.I.M.M. system workshops can go to *www.haneberg-management.com* and follow the H.I.M.M. links for more information. On this Web site, trainers will find information about how to obtain a H.I.M.M. system facilitator's manual and how to lead H.I.M.M. workshops.

Corporate training or speaking events
This author is available to conduct speeches, seminars, and training kickoff workshops. Each speech or workshop is tailored to meet the needs of the participants. Groups may range in size from 5 to 500. For examples, contact information, and rates, visit *www.haneberg-management.com* and click on the H.I.M.M. link.

Start an H.I.M.M. book club
Middle managers interested in using the H.I.M.M. system with several of their peers are encouraged to create a book club. Every other week, meet for a brownbag lunch and discussion of a chapter in the book. The group discussion will carry over into the workday and enhance each participant's

ability to use the H.I.M.M. methods and tools. The book club will also serve as a vehicle for improving peer relationships and communication. Beginning a book club is a great option for middle managers who work for companies without management-training personnel available to facilitate training sessions.

Tell Us What You Think

We would like your feedback! The H.I.M.M. system has been a labor of love developed over the past seventeen years. It will continue to expand and improve over time and as new techniques are tested and proved to be effective. Please drop us a note at *himm@haneberg-management.com* or go to *www.haneberg-management.com* and follow the prompts for H.I.M.M. feedback. Tell us about:

- Success stories—We would like to hear about your middle-manager successes. Please share the H.I.M.M. system methods or tools that have helped the most and why. We may include your experiences in future editions of this book. If we do, you will receive a free copy of the edition.
- Struggles—As a middle manager, what is your greatest challenge? Where has success eluded you? What middle-management techniques have not worked for you?
- Views of middle management—What does high impact middle management look like to you? If you have seen it in action, describe it to us. What does this manager do that is different from the behavior of other middle managers?
- Ideas for future topics—What would you like to see in the next book for middle managers? Are there any other management topics you are interested in reading about?

Your opinions are important and valued. Thank you for your feedback!

Index

About the Author

Lisa Haneberg has taught and coached hundreds of managers during the past seventeen years, including hotel managers, power tool manufacturing department leaders, paper mill union presidents, microchip fabrication shift managers, distribution center leaders, ship captains, division vice presidents, and corporate presidents. Each has benefited from the straightforward solutions to common management maladies she offers. As a manager, management trainer, and coach for companies both large and small, Lisa has held leadership positions focused on manager development and effectiveness. Her expertise includes one-on-one management coaching, management course facilitation, organization development, and business writing. Lisa is a certified master trainer and behavioral assessment interpreter. Management is her passion.